MW00711207

Growing Up in Appalachia

by

Ethel Pritchett Kintner

For

Pam

I wish for you the best life can bring

Ethel Kintner

DORRANCE PUBLISHING CO., INC.
PITTSBURGH, PENNSYLVANIA 15222

All Rights Reserved
Copyright © 1998 by Ethel Pritchett Kintner
No part of this book may be reproduced or transmitted
in any form or by any means, electronic or mechanical,
including photocopying, recording, or by any information
storage or retrieval system without permission in writing
from the publisher.

ISBN # 0-8059-4247-5
Printed in the United States of America

First Printing

For information or to order additional books, please write:
Dorrance Publishing Co., Inc.
643 Smithfield Street
Pittsburgh, Pennsylvania 15222
U.S.A.

Dedication

To my husband,
Elgin P. Kintner, M.D.,
who encouraged me to write my memoirs.
I am presenting
Growing Up in Appalachia
to him for his eightieth birthday, which is
September 5, 1997.

Acknowledgement

I am particularly grateful to those who assisted me in preparing my manuscript. The comments and corrections made by my daughter, Johanna Kintner Bryant, and my good friend, Bertha Kinsinger, were invaluable. I kept my husband, Elgin Kintner, busy adjusting the computer when my arthritic fingers hit the wrong key. This book would never have gotten to Dorrance Publishing Co. Inc. without the encouragement and support of a large, caring, and loving family.

I have a feeling of profound gratitude to Dorrance Publishing Company for the editing, production, promoting, and the printing of my "labor of love." I have appreciated the work of those who supervised my book through the process of editing to printing and binding and those who kept me busy in the marketing details from which I learned so much about promotional efforts and marketing techniques. Thanks to all who labored to produce *Growing Up in Appalachia*.

Contents

Chapter One

Growing Up In Appalachia

Taking steps along life's highway is analogous to a life of growth, changes, activities, accomplishments, disappointments, joys, sorrows, strengths, and weaknesses, all necessary and unavoidable. In this respect, people who live in Appalachia are no different from other people anywhere else in the world. I have, however, observed that the social and cultural lives of people from Appalachia differ according to opportunity and availability of access. The need to survive is basic to humankind. The rugged terrain of the Appalachian Plateau and the lack of generated power did not prevent the gentle and compassionate yet tough and resourceful mountain people from making their inevitable, inestimable "mark."

Despite the region's extensive natural resources and its unbelievable scenic beauty, there are pockets of chronic poverty in Appalachia—especially in coal-mining areas and among the people who live deep in the mountain gorges and in the farmlands of the southern states.

In an effort to describe my steps along the Appalachian Journey, I will begin with a genealogical story of my ancestral line beginning with Jacob Bowman, who immigrated from Germany in the early 1700s.

Jacob Bowman entered the country through Philadelphia, and in time the family tree was laden with children, marriages, and deaths. Admittedly, many migrated westward, while others chose to follow the Appalachian chain that crisscrossed the Allegheny plateau from the Catskill Mountains to the Cumberland Plateau and the Great Smoky Mountains.

Jacob Bowman traveled to Rockingham County, Virginia, with the expectation of bringing his family to Tennessee. Unfortunately, he died before this could be accomplished. His wife, Susannah Milhous Bowman, was energetic, enterprising, bold, and ambitious. Therefore, Susannah made the trip with five children in a Conestoga wagon to the Knob Creek community in Tennessee, where she met and married Isaac Hammer, who built a three-story log house for Susannah and her children. This beautiful old house still stands. It carries the inscription "I.H., 1793." [1] Presently, it is owned by my distant cousins, Sam and Joan Humphrey. The Tennessee Historical Commission has erected a historical marker on the Johnson City to Bristol highway to point out the location.

My relation to the Bowmans is through my father, Reuel B. Pritchett. His mother was Rebecca Ann Bowman. The Pritchetts and the Bowmans, along with other extended family members, belong to the same ancestral line that settled in the Knob Creek settlement northwest of Johnson City, Tennessee. They were hardworking, caring, and sharing people—socially, economically, and religiously. They conquered an environment that in time supported a self-contained community with a distinctive lifestyle of brotherhood and justice. They put down deep roots that allowed Jacob Bowman to be my third great-grandfather. They did not allow the negative tales of pioneer migrants, battles won and lost, or exploitation by the natives to prevent them from living their dream. They bound the past to the present, the distant to the here and now, and their efforts made unknown people important, ordinary places extraordinary, and common things significant.

My husband, Dr. Elgin Kintner, researched and compiled the genealogical data for the Tennessee Historical Society that qualified me as a member of the First Families of Tennessee. The material Elgin submitted is being published in the McClung Historical Collection in Knoxville, Tennessee, with material from all the other families who qualify. Tennessee's 200th year of statehood gives me added incentive to explore my roots which are deeply embedded in Appalachia.

Appalachia is the easternmost part of the United States that extends from New York to Alabama. Even though the Appalachian Plateau is separated by ridges that are long and steep-sided, the ridges are paralleled by flat land, a variety of residential neighborhoods, acres of farm land, and deep valleys, with a variety of historical sites. I took my first steps in a valley between the Appalachian region and the Great Smoky Mountains National Park.

My mother, Ella Poff, and my father Reuel Bowman Pritchett, met while Father was in school at Daleville College, Virginia. Daddy and Mother were married in Mother's home in Christiansburg, Virginia, in 1911. They rode the train to Johnson City and started their life together in a small two-story board-and-batten frame house, designed with wide, thick boards attached perpendicular to the foundation and the framing that created the rafters for

---

[1.] Tennessee Historical Markers, Tennessee Historical Commission, 1972 - I.E. 64—Isaac Hammer, p 83.

the two-story home. The joints between the wide boards were striped with narrow wooden strips to create a refined, finished look. The house was on the small farm that Mother and Daddy bought from Joel Sherfey in the vicinity of the Knob Creek Church of the Brethren. This was where Jacob Bowman, a Brethren minister and the patriarch of family tree, had settled when Tennessee was still the state of Franklin. Presently, the farm house is owned by John Humphrey, the brother of the man who owns Susannah Bowman Hammer's log cabin.

Our farm, the board-and-batten frame house, the log cabin, and the Knob Creek Brethren community were all located in Washington County. I was born on August 28, 1913, and in time two sisters and one brother completed our family of six.

Daddy was a Brethren minister, but his first job after getting married, in addition to farming, was serving as treasurer of the Farmers Exchange in Johnson City.

Today, Johnson City has expanded residentially and commercially to the north and west, but as yet they haven't altered what we knew as "the shady lane"—a short mile through the woods from Grandma and Grandpa Pritchett's house to Reuel B. Pritchett's board-and-batten house. Unfortunately, Grandpa and Grandma Pritchett's farm has been absorbed by Johnson City's commercialism. However, a much-loved landmark still stands—a magnificent chinquapin oak near a spring that still flows with cold, clean water, although Grandpa's log across the stream is no more.

When the dinner bell rang, Grandpa walked to the middle of the log, dipped his hands in the water, washed his face, and moistened his hair. Next, he reached under the springhouse that straddled the stream for his cake of homemade soap, washed his hands and arms all the way to his elbows, then came dripping to the side porch to dry on the roller towel just outside the kitchen. He always combed his hair before he came to the table.

Here I am as a little girl. I was born August 28, 1913.

Chapter Two

The House Where I Was Born

I have fond memories of the Sherfey place, the house where I was born. It was a small house with a tin roof that radiated heat like an inferno, which was less than desirable; fortunately, cross ventilation—windows at both ends of the rooms—helped immeasurably. When it rained, we were lulled to sleep with the pitter-patter of the raindrops.

The farm consisted of thirty-six acres of land: an apple orchard, timberland, garden plots, grapevines, and plant beds that defined the boundary that paralleled Indian Ridge. Mother and Daddy had a ready market for farm produce, and they were very successful in their endeavor.

The floor plan of the house was small: living room, kitchen, and one bedroom downstairs; and two bedrooms upstairs divided by the chimney. The redeeming feature of the house was a ten-foot porch stretching the length of the house that housed the water supply (a cistern). An adjacent woodshed doubled for washing equipment, with a clothesline to hang baby diapers, and storage for the winter's supply of wood.

The porch was unique in that it was framed on the bedroom end of the house. A lot of living was safely, securely, and successfully done on the front porch, with full confidence that we were protected, and safety was never questioned. The porch faced the woodland, and the things I enjoyed most were the patches of May apples, the strawberry patch, and the year-round grapevine swing.

The virgin timber is as beautiful today as it was when I strolled the path to the grapevine swing, and the little pond fed by runoff water, the blooming May apples, and the dugout with burlap drapes. The trees were tall and close enough to the house and the porch to provide shade for the hot summer days.

The house was without electricity and the cleaned, filled, trimmed kerosene lamps on the living room mantle were both ornamental and necessary. The lamp on the table at the head of the stairs was a permanent fixture. The table cloth was one of Mother's many elegant pieces of drawn work made for her hope chest when she was a teenager. Two lanterns hung on hooks from the rafters, one at either end of the porch, provided light for the darkness after sunset and were a field day for the moths and bugs.

The house was heated by a fireplace in the living room and the cook stove in the kitchen. At an early age I was addicted to an open fire. I've always believed that rolling hot flames, the smell of burning wood, and the crackling sounds of glowing embers were in some way therapeutic. They seemed all the more so when I was sitting in a comfortable rocking chair lined with an outing wool-filled comforter recuperating from a sore throat, an inner ear infection, or some other illness that required rest. Mother was a nurse, and she had plenty of practice taking care of her very own.

Gomer, my brother, had repeated attacks of croup at night. An inflammation in the larynx that leads to difficult breathing, croup is accompanied by a strident, harsh, croaking noise which is very frightening for children. I remember how scary it was, but I can never remember that Mother called the doctor; neither did she panic.

Doctor Clark lived on the other side of Indian Ridge. To make a house call he had to ride a horse or come in a buggy, traveling on unpaved roads for several miles. At night, this was very difficult.

Mother was familiar with childhood diseases and knew that in time, sympathetic treatment, loving care, good food, and the rocking chair treatment would be successful. Mother's treatment for earache was drops of warm olive oil in the outer ear canal, plugged with a cotton ball and reinforced with a hot water bottle. For sore throat she had us gargle with warm, mild salt and soda water. For severe tonsillitis Mother swabbed with peroxide. For upper respiratory problems involving the chest or head, she used a hot poultice of Vick's salve.

While playing once, my little red wagon turned over on a harrow spike (a farm implement), and I sustained a severe would on the upper outside of my left leg about two inches below the knee. Mother was familiar with the use of tourniquets, which are placed above the injury to compress the blood vessels to stop the flow of blood. She put a bandage over the laceration and bandaged a splint to my leg below the knee to control movement and bleeding. The scar is proof enough that if this had happened today, a few stitches would have been in order.

Around the turn of the present century, medical practice was improved immeasurably, sanitation in particular; and better nursing skills were developed. Mother took full advantage of both. Antibiotics, vaccinations, and the concept of prevention, as opposed to treatment, had not invaded Mother's world when we were young children. However, she was an expert on the germ theory, sanitation, safety, and good common sense. In fact, scientific medicine was just beginning to make inroads into the medical world in the middle 1930s when I was in nurse's training.

Although Mother resisted superstitious cures and had a disdain for ghost stories, she appreciated the folklore of the early settlers in Tennessee and their efforts to carve a new life out of the wilderness. It was evidenced by our house being built, the land cleared, the well dug, and the cistern being constructed so that surface water would not be a problem. Folklore from the ingenious, self-styled, self-made, self-educated people who carved out the first successful settlements will always be an important part of my heritage. As Mother and Father remembered the humble beginnings of their parents, and as I remember the stories, they were both resourceful and prosperous in the new world.

Moreover, it has remained an unanswered question in my mind how Mother nurtured four small children all alone during the week, planted, tended, and harvested the garden, kept the plant beds producing cuttings for the farmers' market. Daddy stayed in Johnson City during the week and came home on the weekend. I can remember when Daddy came home Friday afternoon, he would bring Grandpa and the garden party would begin. The vegetables that were ready for the Johnson City market were gathered, washed, bundled, and put in trays for an early getaway Saturday morning. Mother would not pull her bedding plants, the tomatoes, sweet potatoes, bell pepper, cabbage, and strawberry cuttings, in the evening. She got up at daybreak and pulled a dozen plants, wrapped them in wet paper, and packed them in moist dirt. This process continued until she had exhausted the supply ready for the market. The last thing Mother would do before Daddy left was to sprinkle the plants with water; and if the sun was shining, she would cover the plants with branches from trees.

The Tennessee seasons are such that farmers can have two or three fresh vegetables on the table six months out of the year. Mother and Daddy were experts at keeping the process moving, even if it required covering the first and last plantings from the frost. Fall vegetables—sweet potatoes, lima beams, beets, cantaloupe, onions, turnips, and green beans—were very much in demand by Johnson City housewives, in addition to grapes, apples, peaches, and watermelon.

Two things stand out in my memory as being extra special in our heavenly domicile. The first was that in the summertime, Mother would let us play outside until the sun sank below the horizon and, many time, until dark. Our chief entertainment was seining for the lightning bugs. We had to have a jar filled so we could climb the dark, enclosed stairway indoors in safety! Incidentally, accidentally, and on occasion, we let a few lightning bugs escape from the jars. The flickering light created a rhythm that encouraged us to join Wynken, Blynken, and Nod.

The other thing was that on Saturday evenings in the summertime, Mother would bathe us and put on our nighties; then she would take her bath and put on her nightgown. At about the time for Daddy to come, sometime between dusk and dark, we would walk the well-beaten path in the woods to meet Daddy. Mother would let us take turns calling for Daddy and listening for the echoing sounds. When he heard us calling, he would call back. The sounds vibrated the leaves to a quivering tremble.

Mother was an excellent housekeeper and an artist with needle and thread, crochet hook, and knitting needles. She made her own clothes, baby clothes, clothing for three daughters, and an occasional shirt for Gomer, the only boy.

In nurturing, Mother operated from the cause and effect principle. In the morning, we were fed and dressed for playing outside, weather permitting, and Mother would have Gomer and me watch after Erlene for short periods of time. Heaven knows what we became preoccupied with, but once when Mother came to check, we couldn't find Erlene anywhere. We looked all around the house, front and back, and it was pretty obvious that Erlene had wandered into the woods. Mother was worried and exhausted when she found Erlene fast asleep, and let the seriousness of the situation serve as an object lesson—when asked to watch baby sister, it was very important that we listen.

Mother's neighbors were few and far between. The Humphreys, father and mother of Sam and John who now own the log cabin and the house where I was born, lived less than a half mile away. However, their house was not visible from where we lived. Grandma and Grandpa Pritchett lived a short mile away on the main road to Johnson City. With the security of a telephone, Mother never once felt that she was unprotected or neglected.

When Gomer and I started school, we walked through the back yard to a path that led up and over Indian Ridge to the school in Boones Creek community. The ridge was covered with papaw trees, and Gomer and I would gather as many as we could and sell them to the students for one penny each.

Boones Creek and Knob Creek were rural communities divided by Indian Ridge with an elevation that provided a natural boundary. As I grew older, I can remember hearing a lot of negative conversation about social, cultural, and economic class difference between the two communities. Some of the unjust prejudices, however, became recognizable when Grandma and Grandpa Pritchett's only daughter, Claudia, married Willie Range from across the "Knob." In time we all learned that Uncle Willie was not an obstacle to the Pritchett and Bowman families, but an asset.

As I write about getting ready for church on Sunday, it sounds complicated and primitive, but to Mother and Daddy it was business as usual. On Sunday morning, Daddy would walk this short mile to Grandma and Grandpa's house. Most of the time, Grandpa would have the horse and buggy ready, and Daddy would come back, and pick up the family for a two-mile ride to the modest, white, wooden Church of the Brethren located in the center of the Knob Creek community. Isaac Hammer had organized the church in 1796. The first structure was a log cabin and was the first Church of the Brethren in Tennessee. My father remembered when the congregation built the new structure, which is the same one I attended when I was a little girl. It has been enlarged and remodeled, and it is still in use today.

Unfortunately, in 1916, Daddy had typhoid fever and was in the Johnson City Hospital for six weeks. Mother was pregnant with Erlene, and she delivered a few weeks after Daddy came home. Daddy recuperated slowly but didn't go back to work until Erlene was a few weeks old. I remember that Johnson City Farmers Exchange brought the record book to the house for Daddy to audit.

It was a sad day during World War I when Mother got a letter about her brother James's injuries, telling her that he would be discharged to a naval hospital in the United States for treatment. When Daddy had recuperated he went to visit Uncle James, but Mother was pregnant with Evelyn and didn't go. I can't remember when Mother and Daddy were notified of his death, but I do remember well the day Uncle James's trunk was unloaded on our front porch. Mother was grateful that he hadn't been on the Titanic, the British ocean liner that sank on its maiden voyage from New York to England.

It is comforting to me to know that the board-and-batten house where I took my first steps is being kept in good repair, polished and groomed in the decor of the original, with all the amenities and desirable features of a small mansion.

My husband, Dr. Elgin Kintner, and I visiting the house where I was born. This photo was taken in 1996.

Chapter Three

Moving One Hundred Miles South

The real purpose for moving in 1919 from the Knob Creek community in East Tennessee to the Oak Grove community 100 miles south was Daddy's career change. He would no longer be treasurer of Farmers Exchange in Johnson City, Tennessee. Instead, he would be farming and shepherding a small Church of the Brethren congregation in the Oak Grove community.

Leaving the Sherfey place and moving to the Carson farm of 160 acres in Jefferson County, Tennessee, was my first experience in moving. I do remember something of the logistics. Daddy used the Farmers Exchange's coach and unloaded large barrels on the porch in which to pack the household furnishings. I can't remember how Daddy got the livestock to the boxcar in Johnson City, but I can remember that we spent the night before our departure with Grandpa and Grandma Pritchett. The next morning we had a buggy ride to Johnson City to meet Daddy and pick up our tickets for White Pine, Tennessee. Grandma held Erlene on her lap and shed buckets of crocodile tears all the way to Johnson City. Mother held Evelyn in her arms with confidence and a resolve that the move would be beneficial to everybody. Mother was sorry about Grandma's abnormal grief, but she did not patronize her and tried to make pleasant conversation about the train ride to our new home. In the final parting Grandpa was loving and considerate. Unfortunately, Grandma became more distraught as Mother and Daddy climbed aboard to find our seats and settle down for the journey. However, Daddy went out to comfort both as best he could before climbing aboard the boxcar to keep things in order for the hundred-mile trip to our new home. All of our belongings were in the boxcar, including a crate of chickens that Grandma had insisted we take along.

At that time, I really didn't know why Daddy rode in the boxcar and we rode coach. I still don't know, but my best guess is that he must have thought the livestock needed some special attention. It was exciting riding on the train, stopping to let passengers off and to pick them up.

Daddy had been to the 140 acres Carson farm several weeks before to inspect the house and make plans for the family's arrival. It seems as though we entered the confines of White Pine at about the middle of the afternoon. Mr. Alley was there with his rubber-tired springboard wagon to collect us. Another conveyance was there to transport the items in the boxcar directly to the house. Daddy supervised the operation, and I remember some discussion about Old Bossy being tied to the tail gate of the wagon. However, Mr. Alley wasted no time in covering the four miles to the two-story brick colonial house where Daddy, Mother, and Evelyn were to spend the night. Somehow, Daddy connected with us in time for a delicious dinner at the Alleys's distinctive vintage home. After dinner two Alley daughters, Mrs. Lemon and Mrs. Rodeffer, came to get Gomer, Erlene, and me. Gomer stayed with the Lemons; they had a Gomer the same age. Erlene and I went with the Rodeffers, and I will never forget how hospitable they were to us. Mother and Daddy kept Evelyn with them even when they went to the house to work. Evelyn was still nursing, and some of the members of the church who lived close to the house came to help care for her.

It became very clear early on that it would take longer than first thought to make the house livable. The Alleys, Lemons, and Rodeffers furnished a little vacant house on the Alleys's farm for us to live in until our house was livable, which was about three weeks. I remember they put straw ticks on the floor for us to sleep on, and that was a lot of fun. Sometimes we slept under the stars. Different families took care of us during the day, and in the evening they brought a meal. Laundry was taken and brought in the same way. To say the least, the church's families were generous in every way before we got into the house and for a long time thereafter.

Moving day finally came. The house was a white, two-story frame, with a conventional, pre-Civil War floor plan: living room, parlor, large eat-in kitchen, walk-in pantry, bedroom with small front porch, screened porch, back porch, and two bedrooms upstairs with large walk-in closets. The house had three fireplaces, one in the living room, one in the parlor, and one in an upstairs bedroom.

The house was located on seven acres of land. Other buildings included the barn, toolshed, smokehouse, summer house, woodshed, and corn crib. The lawn occupied three acres, including the garden. A wet weather ditch divided the back lawn from the farm land and the side lawn from the orchard. The front lawn faced the road with many varieties of evergreens, and deciduous trees were scattered throughout the seven acres.

Mother's rose garden and rows of gladiolus were distinguished by a variety of colors and species. As I write this, memories of cultivating and weeding the garden, mowing the grass, trimming trees, and clipping along the fence rows, trees, and shrubs, seem overwhelming—but somehow it got done!

We lived a short mile from the church and a three-room school with two porches and a long mile from the unique country village of Oak Grove.

The village was distinguished by a population of 500 people. The community was served by two general merchandise stores, a ferry boat across the French Broad River, two doctors' offices, a canning factory, blacksmith shop, grist mill, sawmill, fish market, seamstress, beauty parlor, barbershop, and stock yards.

Oak Grove's three churches—Baptist, Methodist, and Brethren—adorned the pinnacles formed by the French Broad River. Fortunately, they escaped the Tennessee Valley Authority (TVA) construction of a network of hydroelectric power dams for industrial, commercial, and private use.

In general, the Oak Grove community was a farming community. The prosperity of World War I was evidenced by easy money and major investments in land, dairy herds, a cheese factory, macadam roads, and small self-employed manufacturing operations. Agriculture products boosted farm prices considerably from 1914 until the conclusion of war in 1918. Even though the war disrupted the routine of everyday life to some extent and brought the loss of lives to some Tennessee homes, most Tennesseans did not feel the direct impact of the war to the same degree as they did the Great Depression of the 1930s.

During that decade, the people of Appalachia experienced remorse and despair that shook the very foundations on which they had based their lives. Never before had so many people in Oak Grove been so helpless, drowning as it were in a whirlpool of conflicting circumstances and ideas. To be sure, the community was rocked by its pockets of poverty, poor schools, unemployed sharecroppers, and faltering economy. The Depression crowded in upon hundreds who had formerly made a respectable living, who suddenly found themselves faced with depressed markets, falling prices, bank closings, and foreclosures. In time a political regime sought solutions and made some long overdue changes.

In the early 1920s Alf Taylor, a Democrat, was elected governor and handily won three consecutive terms. His accomplishments during the next twelve years were noteworthy: he paved thousands of miles of state roads; converted Reelfoot Lake into a state game and fish reserve; supported a movement for a national park in the Great Smoky Mountains and took the first step toward land acquisition for the park by purchasing the Little River tract in 1925; instigated state-supported high schools; appointed a professionally trained state superintendent of schools provided an eight-month school term; standardized the licensing of teachers; created school libraries; and required teachers to train for two years in normal school. Normal schools were located in Johnson City, Murfreesboro, and Memphis. In the 1920s, high schools were built in each school district.

Unfortunately, during Alf Taylor's last term of office the General Assembly passed the Butler Bill, which outlawed the teaching of evolution. Almost immediately John Thomas Schopes, a young biology teacher from Dayton, Tennessee, was arrested for violation of the new law. Many people believed the law was an attack on Christianity. Charles Darwin's theory of evolution was particularly offensive to the fundamentalist faith which adhered to a narrow interpretation of the Bible. The trial was long and arduous; most major newspapers reported the proceedings. Dayton became famous and Tennessee became the "Monkey State" until finally Scopes was exonerated. The Butler Law remained on the statute book until its repeal in 1967.

As I grew older, I became more aware of the distance between the economic status of people in the Oak Grove community and that of the unfortunate poor within the state. The Great Depression, however, was no respecter of persons. From the most remote coves of the mountainous region of East Tennessee to the bustling metropolitan areas of Memphis, some five hundred miles away, the enduring lesson of contrast and compare experienced—"Now you have it, now you don't."

Fortunately, our family did not suffer the humiliation of a foreclosure on the farm. I am not sure of our losses when the bank closed. I am sure that the loss of income came from the drop in market economy. Daddy sold wheat and corn for twenty-five cents a bushel. He was forced to shoot the calves; it was not profitable to feed them for the veal market.

We were not used to "store-bought" clothing because Mother made our dresses, petticoats, panties, suits, and jackets. Similarly, Mother brought bleached and unbleached muslin by the bolt for clothing and other household uses. During the Depression she used feed sacks in the same way, for petticoats, panties, curtains, towels, aprons, dishcloths, nightshirts, pajamas, and roller-towels for the kitchen. Some of the sacks were soft and bleached to a snow white, and Mother made blouses trimmed in rickrack for all the girls.

Daddy and Mother continued to farm. We had a variety of garden vegetables six months out of the year. Mother canned and preserved berries, fruits, and vegetables. Daddy continued to fatten and butcher more hogs than we could use. We boarded two engineers from the Douglas Lake construction over the French Broad River for more than a year. Later on, we boarded reporters from the *National Geographic* magazine many times during the Great Depression and World War II.

We had potatoes, squash, sweet potatoes, and pumpkins that would keep until spring. We had chickens and eggs the year round. Mother baked large loaves of yeast bread twice a week. She would always bake small rolls, cupcakes, and cookies for school lunches and the boarder's lunch boxes. We had an abundance of food, good heat in winter time, plenty of outing flannel, and homemade quilts and feather beds in which to snuggle at night. I confess that I enjoyed the Appalachia country setting in the valley between

Great Smoky Mountains and the Cumberland Gap. In fourth grade civics class I learned that the necessities of life are food, clothing, and shelter. I confess that, by today's standards, we were without the luxuries of life. We had very little money. We did not have electricity, a furnace, or air-conditioning. I did my homework at night by the light of a kerosene lamp. I took my bath in a galvanized tub. I washed clothes on a rub board, swept the house with a broom, and ironed clothes with a smoothing iron heated on the cook stove or in front of an open fire.

The Tennessee Valley Authority (TVA), established in the early 1930s to benefit farmers and non-farmers alike, was a direct response to the Great Depression. As time passed this agency touched the lives of all of Tennessee's residents in five basic areas: production of electricity, river development, flood control, agricultural improvement, and comfort to farm families.

Furthermore, the people of the Oak Grove community had been devastated when water from the Douglas Dam across the French Broad River flooded the foundations of buildings in Oak Grove Village. The buildings and houses were demolished. Thousands of acres of bottomland were covered by water. Many of the flooded farms had been handed down by families for generations. Finally, the evicted relocated, the homeless found shelter, and those left undisturbed by the TVA were complacently waiting for the promised results of the inconvenience, destruction, and humiliation of the project in the first place.[2]

[2] Deb Mulrey, We Had Everything But Money; *Priceless Memories of the Great Depression*; 1992, Reiman Publication. L.P.; Greendale WI, p.7

We moved to Jefferson County, Tennessee, in the fall of 1919. This is the front of the house.

This is the back view of the house.

The Pritchett children. Standing: Erlene, Gomer, and Ethel. Seated: Evelyn.

In time, an unexpected and extraordinary economic development came to the Oak Grove community and the state of Tennessee as a result of the electric switch, which was equivalent to the luxuries of life, and opposed to the necessities of life.

In my lifetime, I have experienced the transformation from pioneers' plows to symphonic sounds; from buggies to automobiles; from wars dividing the nations to innovative ways of providing new methods, practices, divides, transportation, communications; and construction of paths, trails, lakes, parks, railroads, highways. Now the technology-driven information superhighway dominates commercial and industrial development in Tennessee and around the world.

Clancy Strock described the Great Depression thusly: "Theirs was the generation that went from outhouses to outer space, from kerosene lamp to computer, from straw mattresses to supersonic jets."

Chapter Four

My Life As a Teenager

My childhood was warm, cheerful, and busy. As a teenager, a few years passed before I recognized that the future for me was almost here. The question frequently flashed through my mind, "What am I going to do when I grow up?" Later, I realized this was a normal question for teenagers to ask. However, the Depression was still with us, and I was well aware of the limited possibilities it imposed. In making the transition from grade school to Maury High School in Dandridge, the county seat, about five miles southwest of Oak Grove, I learned that experiences of the Great Depression varied with each family.

Mother and Daddy survived the years between 1930 and 1940 by persevering, working hard, being resourceful, and managing well. They knew many families in our community who had much less, and they were resigned to make the best of a situation over which they had no control. They were not bitter, and we were made to believe that we were privileged and special in that we could work, learn, and endure gracefully.

The farm work was made easy because farming was a family affair. Assignments were not necessary; we were not told to do specific things since caper charts were not in vogue in those days. Farm life operated on self-evident principles: If we wanted to eat, we needed to gather the eggs, milk the cows, and feed the hogs; if we needed hot water in the reservoir behind the stove, it had to be filled; if we wanted to keep warm, we had to have wood for the kitchen stove and fireplaces.

When we were in high school we rode the bus to and from school. We walked one mile to and from the bus stop. We got home between four and five o'clock in the afternoon, changed clothes, and did the chores that automatically flow from a life on the farm.

The in-house chores belonged to the women in the household. At an early age I milked cows, turned the separator to remove the cream from the milk, and churned the cream to make butter. By necessity, I learned to cook and sew before I took home economics in high school. Mother had confidence that under Mrs. Rankin, my home economics teacher, I would refine finishing touches in sewing and bought nice materials for me to work with. The princess dress line was very fashionable at that time. I made a navy blue dress with a lace collar and cuffs, a kitchen smock, and a party apron. We were given the opportunity to make something for the Tennessee State Fair, and I won first place with a baby layette. As a junior, much to my surprise Mother suggested that next year I could make clothing appropriate for college—skirts and blouses. That was the first time Mother had mentioned education beyond high school.

Through our last few years in grade school and high school, the family experienced health problems of some magnitude. My sister, Evelyn, and I had diphtheria. Dr. Huggins vaccinated us but not before I had been sick for several days. After months of illness, I was left with an abscess on my neck that had to be excised. My brother, Gomer, was critically ill for weeks with typhoid fever. Tonsillectomies were performed on all of us girls in a makeshift hospital upstairs over a drugstore in White Pine. The surgeons and nurses came from Fort Sanders hospital in Knoxville. Appendectomies were performed on all of us girls at home by the medical crew from Morristown. Mother had serious surgery twice at Fort Sanders hospital in Knoxville.

My sister, Erlene, was accident-prone: cuts, bruises, stitches, and torn clothing from climbing fences and trees were situations that she endured without a whimper. However, she had an encounter at the barn when the cistern that was two-thirds filled with water literally made it possible for Mother to save her life. As I remember, we were playing hide and seek when Erlene attempted to jump across the exposed opening to the cistern and missed. I went screaming to the house for Mother. Although I could not answer Mother when she asked me what happened, Mother followed me to the section of the barn that housed the cistern, which had galvanized pipe that conducted the water to which Erlene was holding on for dear life. Mother laid flat, held on to something with one hand, reached down into the cistern, grabbed Erlene by one arm, and brought her out. Mother turned her upside down and emptied her lungs of water, then laid her flat on her stomach, head down, until her vital signs stabilized. Daddy wasn't home at the time, but I remember Mother telling Daddy about the near fatal accident.

Unfortunate but true, after Erlene had finished one year of nurse's training at Baptist Hospital in Nashville, she came down with pulmonary pleurisy. She came home and the treatment was one year in bed. Fortunately, at the end of the year, all symptoms were negative, and she was readmitted and finished with honors.

As a teenager, I was not aware of the competitiveness between the political parties until President Roosevelt won the election in 1933. One of his many promises to the people during the Depression became reality through the Civilian Conservation Corps also know as the CCC camps.

The CCC provided warm beds, clean clothes, hot meals, and meaningful work to three million unemployed men. An enrolled person received thirty dollars a month, twenty-five of which was sent back to his family. With room, board, clothes, medical care, and vocational training provided, some men found camp life so pleasant that they stayed for as long as six years.

The masonry work along the highway in the Great Smoky Mountains was the work of CCC men. They helped to build the road, cleared the trails, fought fires, created beautiful campgrounds, and built dams and bridges. Much of their work is visible in the park today. In addition to food, clothing, and shelter, the men were exposed to recreation, swimming pools, and reading material, as well as the chance to take classes in a separate education building. Boys who improved their education and skills were given promotions. Assistant leaders were paid thirty-six dollars a month, and a leader made forty-five dollars a month. I've heard it said many times that CCC workers went in as boys and came out as men!

It is hard to evaluate the positive effects the Civilian Conservation Corps had on the morale of the men and the families from which they came. I do know for sure that it kept some of the families in the Oak Grove community out of the poor house.

The Great Depression encouraged some strengths as well as revealing weaknesses. As a teenager, I made some observations: People became more compassionate, helped themselves overcome problems, and taught many others a better way of life. People were willing to do with less and encouraged pride, bravery, and determination. They endured hard work but had fun, and they were more neighborly. The Great Depression offered hope to thousands of people through deeds of kindness and humble generosity.

Those times are as vivid to me today as they were when a slender spirited woman walked past our house at six o'clock every Monday morning to a neighbor's house, a distance of four miles, to do the week's laundry. She received twenty-five cents for a day's work. On the way home, she stopped at Leeper's store and bought beans. As she passed our house, Mother gave her bacon and occasionally a loaf of bread. Mother felt kindly toward her and sorry that she was so destitute: her husband was unemployed, and they had three children. When the CCC camps became a reality, their son signed up. The mother continued to do laundry for the neighbor lady and she let Mother know she had been a good neighbor and thanked her for the gifts of food. She said to Mother, "I will be getting some money every month from my son in the CCC camp." She was a proud mother!

Although the Depression sometimes challenged my ingenuity, I recall many delightful memories. The community people never failed to socialize. They visited with one another, had quilting bees, made apple butter, husked corn, and had meetings concerning community needs. Teenagers had fun with popcorn parties, ice cream socials, picnics, box suppers, and Halloween parties.

Once, we had a Halloween party at our home in the barn. Our parties were always a family affair where everybody participated in the preparation, entertainment, and cleanup. The horse stalls in the barn were cleaned to fertilize garden plots in the spring of the year. Two stalls near the front of the barnyard were sanitized with shocks of fodder around the four walls, and clean bales of straw were placed in front of the fodder. The driveway was swept clean and given the same treatment as the stalls. Bags of multi-colored leaves were brought from the woods to carpet the floor of the stables and the driveway. Daddy literally swept the barnyard and distributed bales of straw, shocks of fodder, and pumpkins in an artistic fashion. To pierce the darkness, lanterns were hung from the rafters inside the barn and on posts in the barnyard.

Mother baked eight loaves of bread, and she had a small brass kettle of apple butter brewing on the kitchen stove. As people gathered, they were led to the totally dark stable for initiation: pumpkins had been sliced in half, and the insides, seeds and all, were smeared on faces and hands. All twenty-five guests proceeded to the next stall to experience the ghosts and goblins. Screams and laughter provided good entertainment until all had been through the initiation process.

Different guests chose to pitch horseshoes, bob for apples, or walk in a burlap sack tied above the knee the distance of the barn lot—competing for the best time. In the middle of the barnyard sat a barrel of popcorn seasoned with butter and salt, to be eaten at will. As the evening wore on, Mother served the apple butter and homemade bread with hot cider. At the stroke of midnight, the party was over. My dictionary defines a party as "A gathering of people to have a good time." I believe our Halloween party met that definition.

As a teenager, I was aware of the social and economic conditions of Appalachia, as opposed to other regions that had affordable electricity. In all honesty, social customs and economic conditions are directly related to being able to read. Reading is the foundation on which all other education takes place. When President Roosevelt signed the Tennessee Valley Authority Act on May 18, 1933, he understood the power of an electric switch and what it would do for the homesteaders, farmers, homeowners, and housewives. I did not understand how the annual per capita income of $168 per year in the Tennessee Valley region could be improved. The labor force was unskilled, and the literacy rate was low. Over fifty percent of the people farmed, and the sharecroppers who worked for a share of the yield were often malnourished, poorly housed, and without medical care.

I was content with my country upbringing, partly because I had the necessities of life, but I was nevertheless distressed over the poverty in Appalachia. I felt that people grow and prosper in relation to their birthright. My birthright was different from that of the sharecropper, yet we were both deprived because of undeveloped resources awaiting benevolent action. There is an old adage that says: "If man is hungry, give him a fishing pole and he will eat for life." The CCC men and the electrical switch exemplified the truth of this statement.

It was a long, tedious, lonesome road out of The Great Depression that had paralyzed the United States. The creation of the Great Smoky Mountains national park, authorized in 1926 and officially established in 1934, proved very beneficial, as did the establishment of the Tennessee Valley Authority in 1933 for the purpose of building dams that would produce electricity by water power to Manhattan Project—the secret operation of World War II at Oak Ridge.

In spite of Roosevelt's popularity and his "New Deal" aimed at overcoming the disastrous Depression, he had critics, and many of his laws were bitterly opposed. Pitched political battles were fought over TVA's entry into the electric business in competition with private industry. Roosevelt's promise to rescue the people from poverty was long in coming, and people became discouraged and fearful. To bring the government into direct participation with people's lives meant a political disaster to some people.

For example, my father waited eight years hoping that within the near future we would be able to hook on to the electric service line that was being constructed in our community. After having our house wired we waited another twelve years.

What postponed electrical service for farmers and homeowners was World War II. Then, something happened in the east Tennessee hills unlike anything that had ever happened before; the city of Oak Ridge was shrouded in secrecy, and the Manhattan Project constructed the atomic bomb that ended World War II.

After the war, rationing ended. People could buy new cars. Electricity came to home owners, farmers, and new businesses. Jobs were created when the TVA's dam construction attracted industry, and entrepreneurs took advantage of the cheap power that resulted from President Roosevelt's "New Deal."

Increased prosperity also meant more leisure time for Tennessee Valley residents. The TVA responded with more extensive recreational development, which in turn made the area a retirement Mecca. Because of the work performed there during the war years, Oak Ridge became one of the most famous towns in the world. Today, Oak Ridge National Laboratory is known as the laboratory that developed the process to separate the plutonium that fueled the reactor from the uranium that produced the atomic bomb. In addition, Oak Ridge is also known around the world as center of a broad range of science and technology beneficial to humankind.

As a teenager, I knew very little about the short-range or long-term effects of the new agencies that made the impossible possible. However, FDR's vision of TVA is an example of what government can do for its people in times of economic hardship. It was not a giveaway program; it was a program that involved people in the development of their own natural resources for the good of all.

My mother and father, Ella Poff Pritchett and Reuel Bowman Pritchett

Chapter Five

My College Days

As I browsed through memorabilia, I found the invitation to my high school commencement exercise (class of 1933). The most amazing thing was the stamp of one and a half cents on the envelope. When I think of the discrepancy between "now" vs. "then," it begs the question about current conditions of money, worth, college expenses, cultural mores, technological advances, and how students are going to be served in our rapidly changing economy and environment. The best that we can hope for is to educate our youth. They are our most valuable resource in this world.

I do not crave a competitive, advantage in pursuing the biggest and best of everything when in the past necessities seemed so satisfying. But I do covet the best for all our students. Similarly, Dr. Paul Bowman, President of Bridgewater College, a cousin of my father, described the financial circumstances at the college when I was a freshman in 1933. In Dr. Bowman's own words:

> There is perhaps no more complex problem confronting the college than that of the worthy, talented, and ambitious student who is without the necessary means for meeting his college expenses. The demand for assistance is beyond our power to supply. We have been creating limited work opportunities on the campus. We have also established some scholarships and acquired a few loan funds for the benefit of this class of students. But with all of this we still turn away literally hundreds of students who deserve the advantages of higher education. [3]

[3.] Wayland, Francis Fry, Bridgewater College, *The First Hundred Years,* 1880-1980, Brunswick Publishing Corp. 1993

Most of the students who attended Bridgewater College in the 1930s came under Dr. Paul's evaluation of need. Moreover, Dr. Paul aspired to enlarge the geographical area from which the student body came, and he spent his summers recruiting students. He visited the states surrounding Bridgewater College, which is located in the northwest part of Virginia.

Our home was his last stop before school started. The French Broad Church of the Brethren was known as the most southern church in the District. Dr. Paul spent the night with us as he had many times before and he was more than pleased with the response he got in the state of Tennessee—especially around Johnson City and Jonesborough. Most of the students who signed up were young people whom I had known through the youth fellowship programs in the churches and summer camp. Daddy and Mother had already decided that I would go to Bridgewater if I could get a job that would pay half the tuition. Students were forbidden a scholarship if they were included in a work program. My brother Gomer had attended Bridgewater the year before, and we were both there in fall of 1933. Money for a college education was hard to come by during the depression years— I quickly learned that my parents were not the only parents who sacrificed to give their children a chance.

I was excited over the prospect of going to Bridgewater. I spent the summer working on the farm, shucking sweet corn at the canning factory, and working as a timekeeper for the canning factory at Oak Grove, all of which paid ten cents an hour.

I spent considerable time going through what I had and what I needed in the way of clothing for college. By the end of August I had earned twelve dollars. Mother and I decided I needed a good church-going, light-weight wool dress, a pair of shoes, and two pairs of hose. This decision created quite an adventure. I took the bus from Dandridge to Knoxville to shop at Miller's store on Gay Street. I chose navy blue wool for the dress material and white linen for detachable collar and cuffs. I remember I paid ten cents for the pattern. The collar was larger than a "Peter Pan" collar, but the top was otherwise plain. The skirt had box pleats all around. Good wool could be bought for two dollars a yard; I paid four dollars for my shoes, and I have forgotten what I paid for my hose, but I had enough change left over to return home.

Even though I had taken home economics in high school, Mother helped me interface the cuffs and collar so they would look crisp when laundered and stay in place when attached.

I was a little naive about if I should have, or what I should have in the way of formal wear. Mother and Daddy seemed to know—perhaps they had discussed this with Dr. Paul. I was told that Bridgewater had Lyceum lectures in the evenings once a month requiring dress up and/or formal wear.

This was my first need for a formal long dress, and I was proud and pleased. I chose a long pink silk crepe dress with an ostrich plume shawl and appropriate accessories.

It was a great day when Daddy drove me, with my trunk, in the horse carriage to board the train for Johnson City, where I would join some of the other students going to Bridgewater college. Uncle Joe Bowman met me and we had to tie my trunk to the running board of his Model T Ford. I spent the night with Uncle Joe and Aunt Ottie. The next morning we had to get two trunks to Johnson City because their son Charles was also going to Bridgewater. They used what they called the "horse-drawn delivery coach." They were farmers and had farm produce to deliver to customers in Johnson City several times a week. They also ran a dairy farm, for which they had year-round customers.

Four students—Charles Bowman, Evelyn Clark, Frank Isenburg, and myself—rode the train to Mount Crawford where we were met by one of Bridgewater's upperclassmen. The college truck collected our trunks, and I got mine in time to start unpacking before I went to dinner. All students who had signed up for dining room duty were to report to the kitchen the next morning at six o'clock.

I admit that my work schedule, which included dining room duty for three meals a day, shelving books in the library three times a week, and working as an assistant matron of Yount Hall for three months, was time-consuming. The sophisticated title of "assistant matron" meant cleaning bath tubs, wash basins, commodes, and sweeping floors. My work schedule took up an enormous amount of valuable time.

In addition to classes and work assignments, I was a member of the Gamma Gamma Club, which was made up of students whose parents had attended Bridgewater College. I was a cabinet member of the Brethren Young People's Department. On weekends we would present programs to other organizations, youth groups, and churches. We were also in charge of the Sunday evening programs on the campus. In spring we would visit many Brethren churches, giving information about Bridgewater College. We also had a visitation day on the campus for prospective students in which the student body and faculty participated. On a regular basis, I conducted a Sunday School class for the black children in the community. Many of the parents worked in the college. Furthermore, I was a member of the Bridgewater College Literary Club. I enjoyed the meetings, but unfortunately, I could not find the time to give a program. I was always grateful that they depended on volunteers and many members were willing to review a book or read an interesting story or give a pantomime. My literary knowledge, however, was improved immeasurably because I belonged to the club and attended the programs regularly.

I found college work demanding and exciting. However, I had one catastrophic experience the first semester that almost did me in: I failed chemistry. This was the first time that I had ever failed a course. I did not have a foundation in chemistry; it was not taught in Maury High School which I had attended, and I was unable to put the "building blocks" of college chemistry together on the final exam. I had asked for help, but the lab assistants didn't have extra time to spend. Afterward, I realized I should have been more aggressive and talked to the professor. However, this was a good lesson to learn early on!

Nevertheless, I took this problem to the head office and asked if I could take biology the second semester, for which I had a good foundation. They let me know this was an unusual request, and that the biology class was halfway through the book. I told them that I would schedule biology the first semester next year and complete the course. After days of waiting my request was granted, but they were very clear about the grade: "You will not get a grade until you have finished the course!" This pleased me very much, but the reply was a little curt. The professor in biology felt he had to make some remark about an extra student in last semester's class, and he was less than graceful or complimentary. Nevertheless, I was able to display some intelligence about the subject matter in biology, my home work was interesting, and after the first test the hurt that I had experienced in failing chemistry began to disappear.

During my second year at Bridgewater, even though I was a sophomore I felt like an upperclassman. I knew a little bit more about what was going on. I was taking core courses with the expectation of being a school teacher. However, during the second semester, I became interested in nursing. I was studying psychology: plain, general, child, and educational courses. Human behavior, sick or well, became very interesting to me. Upon investigating the opportunities in nursing, I began to talk about my interest in nursing to my friends. When school was out, I made no promises to anybody about seeing them in the fall. But there was one thing that I had decided to do, and that was to pay my own expenses whether I taught school or went into nursing.

When I got home, I investigated school teaching. At that time, one could teach in elementary school with a two-year college certificate. I put my application in, but I didn't hear for several weeks—in fact, until just a few weeks before school started. I was offered a seven-month school in Cocke County, on a mud road, in the heart of Appalachia, fifteen miles north of Newport, Tennessee for one dollar a day. The arrangements created more problems for me than it solved. After board and room and an occasional weekend at home, I could have gone in debt instead of saving enough for one year's tuition or a summer term at East Tennessee State in Johnson City, Tennessee.

My uncle, Roy Poff (mother's brother), lived in Roanoke, Virginia, and he was acquainted with my situation. So he invited me up to visit the hospitals. He was a business man and advised me that nurses were in demand with wages which were equal to or more than school teachers. I went for a visit and I was impressed. There was one problem—the new class at the Roanoke General Hospital started the next week. Decisions were made, and I was challenged by a new set of experiences.

Me and my roommate, Nellie Compton, at Bridgewater College, 1935.

Chapter Six

From College to Nurse's Training

It is hard to recall my feelings, expectations, and a secret promise to myself about the change of events from college to nursing training.

When I visited Roanoke General Hospital one week before the new class started, I filled out an application and toured the hospital. I was given material about the hospital's service to the community and the requirements for nurses and interns. I was impressed that the doctors took care of the indigent free of charge. The doctors on the staff felt that they constituted a public service to the community, from which the community benefitted immeasurably.

By the time I got home, I was notified that I had been accepted. This created a big change in my needs for the next three years in regard to finances, clothing, and room and board, and also in relation to my social life and the clientele with whom I would be associated. As plans changed and time passed, I became confident that I had made the right choice.

I got a loan for two or three hundred dollars from Daddy—equivalent to $1,700 or $2,550 in 1990. There was no tuition, but I had transportation costs traveling to Roanoke and some commuting costs going across town to Roanoke College for classes. I had to buy books and notebooks for course work, and uniforms, shoes, and hose according to the student dress code for trainees.

The other thing that attracted me to Roanoke General Hospital was the free room, board, and laundry and a stipend of $10 a month. A benevolent patient had been impressed with the nursing care at Roanoke General Hospital during her prolonged stay and at her death left an endowment to be used for the student nurses. Every time I picked up my monthly $10 check, I felt warmed by her generosity. Incidentally, that was equivalent to

$85 a month in 1990. Fortunately, this stipend was all the money that I needed for the next three years.

I was the last student to be accepted for the fall class and the last student to arrive. The matron met me at the door and took me to a single room on the second floor of the nurses' home. She explained that since I was an "uneven number," I would live alone. I assured her that was fine. Having missed the early morning get-acquainted meeting, I was informed about the week's schedule posted in the classroom. I was also given instruction about the fitting room for shoes, hose, and uniforms. I ran into some of my classmates, and they were able to bring me up-to-date on what went on the day before I arrived. They acquainted me with some of the rules, but were quick to add, "We will hear more about rules, conduct, and decorum in the weeks to follow." And we did.

The program was planned to graduate a class each year and admit a class every six months. Vacations of two weeks were rotated for students from all three classes during the summer months.

The packet of material delineating the probation period included the nurse's code. All of the girls had to be physically fit and participate in some kind of physical exercise twice a week. None of the girls were overweight. Once a month we were checked for weight loss or weight gain. In the third month of the probation period, I was assigned to the 10 P.M. nightly "chow line" for a large, fortified, vanilla shake. I was not the only one in full uniform trying to maintain the weight that the nurse's code considered satisfactory. Furthermore, some were assigned to the diet dining room for weight loss. Our graduation picture, with belts of fresh flowers around our middles, is living proof that the waistlines were kept in check.

Only single white females were accepted for nurse's training at the Roanoke General. All were high school graduates. In my class, two had taught school, and one had been the secretary in the school from which she had graduated. Three students were from Roanoke, three were from out-of-state, and the rest were from Virginia.

I was unfamiliar with the upperclassmen's activities, but they looked important to me as they were giving orders, taking orders, and administering treatments to sick people. However in a very short time I became more familiar with the expectations of a student nurse on probation, commonly referred as a "probe."

By Monday morning September 14, 1936, per instruction of Miss Daisy Donner, director of nursing at Roanoke Hospital, the new class of eleven probes was in uniform at 6 o'clock in the lobby at the nurses' residence filled with curiosity and waiting for a verdict.

Monday morning was the first time that I had met Miss Donner. She was coolly cordial, but she did tell us a little bit about what we were going to do for the day. She took us on a tour of the hospital, and we arrived in time for the changing of the guards—the night shift reporting to the day shift. As we progressed from floor to floor, we saw supply rooms, a pharmacy, the emergency room, hopper rooms, the linen storage and laundry room, the dining rooms for student nurses and for graduate nurses, an auxiliary kitchen on each floor, the delivery room, the operating room, the nursery, the x-ray, laboratory, the sterilizer, and the morgue.

Before the day was over, we also saw the discharging and admitting of a patient, a room equipped appropriately for a sick patient, a well-equipped classroom in the nurses' residence, and the text book, *Fundamentals of Nursing*, that would be our bible for the three months of probation.

We spent many hours on nursing techniques: learning how to admit and discharge patients; to chart progress or the lack of progress; give medications, enemas, douches, back rubs, morning bath, and evening care; and practicing how to give hypodermics, take temperatures, and check pulse and blood pressure on one another. During that time we read about other procedures that were demonstrated in the classroom. However Miss Donner was committed to having us see for ourselves the complicated procedures executed by professionals. We would go to the floor for "show and tell."

Passing both a written examination and a physical examination and demonstrating different nursing procedures were prerequisites to the capping ceremony that formed the foundation for a three-year program for a graduate nurse. This was a very exciting time for all of us. Our capping exercise symbolized that we had satisfactorily mastered the rudimentary elements of nursing.

We no longer had to report to Miss Donner's classroom in the nurses' residence. Instead, we reported to different floors to work in teams of three: a senior nurse, a junior nurse, and a sophomore nurse to care for patients. The hospital also had three supervisors who rotated to give help and advice and see that everything was running according to doctors' orders.

All nurses worked twelve hours a day, with thirty minutes off for breakfast, lunch, and dinner. Sophomores had three classes a week in the evening at Roanoke College from seven to nine P.M. taught by the doctors, juniors had two classes a week, and seniors had one class a week. Additionally, we could be asked by Miss Donner, any one of the supervisors, or the doctors to work on special projects: reports, readings, assignments, demonstrations and/or new procedures, and treatments or medications that were being used for a specific disease.

The staffing patterns for Roanoke General Hospital maximized the skills and knowledge of the girls in the three-year nursing program. Senior girls worked as charge nurses, rotating through all the services with two circulating supervisors available for support and help. The fine line that separated a senior nurse from a charge nurse on the floor included efficiency, accuracy, good judgement, stability, and attitudes in dealing with the many systems at work in a hospital.

By the time the first-year girls had progressed through supervised practice, experience on the floor, and a years' course work, they were valuable supportive help.

The junior girls had more responsibility on the floor. They were able to do all the procedures, including injections, monitoring and changing intravenous solutions, giving medications, taking blood pressures, and caring for surgical recovery patients using sterile techniques, and in general they were indispensable in the chain of health care workers.

Many patients who were cared for in the '30s were sick with diseases that are uncommon today: communicable diseases, tuberculosis, typhoid fever, syphilis, gonorrhea, pneumonia, osteomyelitis, hookworm, roundworm, pleurisy, otitis, and malnutrition. Surgical patients were cared for without the benefit of a recovery room or intensive care. The recovery period for a surgery patient was eight to ten days. Maternity patients were kept in bed for a week.

During my three years of training, much progress was made in sanitation and specialization. Once a week clinic days were supervised by a public health nurse. This was especially beneficial to expectant mothers and small children. As sophisticated diagnostic techniques were developed, nursing specialties were developed: surgical nurse, pediatric nurse, private duty nurse, obstetrical nurse, and general duty nurse. Today the number continues to grow.

During my senior year, two things occurred that I shall never forget. First, antibiotics for gonorrhea and syphilis patients were unbelievably successful, so successful that we had a sudden drop in census.

The second benefitted nurses immeasurably. As a matter of hospital policy, the hospital staff, the board of directors, and the nursing supervisors, separated housekeeping duties from nursing duties. As nurses became better educated and more proficient, there was much confusion over nurses; work as opposed to housekeeping, orderly duties, and maintenance work in hopper rooms where everything was sterilized and where surgical packs were assembled for individual doctors and for different surgical procedures. All during my training there was much talk about the work ethic for nurses. The twelve-hour shift had been maintained at Roanoke General from the beginning. In the fall of 1940, the hospital honored the legislation that nurses work only eight-hour shifts. This literally shook the foundation on which we walked. Naturally, nurses were overjoyed. Implementing the legislation was not so easy. Some people felt intimidated, but in time it became the rule, not the exception.

The three years that I spent at Roanoke General were very meaningful years in my life. After having read the textbooks about medical problems and having the doctors answer questions during class period, explaining more fully the cause, treatment, and prognosis of a disease, and citing examples in the hospital for student nurses to follow and observe, I could not have been more pleased. These were unequaled learning tools. I always read the patient's history, diagnosis, and treatment from the chart. Serving three months on each service—medical, surgical, obstetric, pediatric, nursery, laboratory, operating room, delivery room, and emergency room—gave me the opportunity to learn that good medical practice is truly a matter of life and death. I felt privileged to share in the excitement.

I had mixed feelings of joy, regret, and relief while working my last day at Roanoke General Hospital. The thoughts that came to me surprised me very much. I recalled the day that I was given the opportunity to be measured for the standard Roanoke General graduate nurse's white uniform, and then I remembered that I would no longer sit down to three prepared meals a day that had been no effort of mine. I would no longer pick up a pack of washed, mended, starched, and ironed uniforms that I did not do, and I would no longer live without paying rent. However, when I did move out of the nurses' residence, I lived with Uncle Roy, Aunt Hazel, Betty Lee, and Jean Poff until I took my state boards and got a job.

Uncle Roy drove me to Richmond, Virginia, the day before the state boards, ushered me to my hotel room, and wished me well. I spent two days taking six exams a day. The real joy came when the exams were over and I was safely on a bus back to Roanoke. I truly had mixed feelings about how I had performed on the exams; but some of the questions had made some sense and I lived with hope.

The real relief came when Daisy Darner, A.B., R.N., Educational Director, called me over to get my R.N. certification. She also offered me a job as supervisor with a salary of $120 a month. This was equivalent to $1,020 in 1990. I thanked Daisy Darner and went to work on the following Monday morning. In time, I found a place to live close to Uncle Roy and Aunt Hazel's home. The streetcar came to the corner, and I was in business.

After a few months, I decided to join the ranks of private duty nurses. I had heard the remark from graduate nurses, "One's nursing training is never over until she has served a term with Dr. Green in the Blue Ridge Mountains of Virginia."

One morning, after I had worked all night but before I had gone to bed, the phone rang and it was Dr. Green's office in Ferrum, Virginia, wanting me to do some private nursing duty for him. His office was in Ferrum, Virginia, twenty miles south of Roanoke. I had no idea of what I was in for, but I looked forward to joining the ranks of nurses who had experienced the hollows, hills, and deep gorges of this section of the Appalachia.

I had just been dismissed from a three-week case, and I had immediately called to have my name posted on the register. Being bound by the nursing ethic (if you are not working and are needed, you work), I told Dr. Green I would be glad to come. He sent his son for me at 2 P.M. for the thirty-mile ride to Ferrum. Dr. Green's office was in the drugstore. I observed one sidewalk on the side of the drugstore and a few other buildings that the sidewalk also served. Dr. Green came out when we drove up and told me that we were switching cars because of the mud roads. His son loaded my bags into a truck that would supposedly climb a tree if necessary. Dr. Green invited me in and acquainted me with the patient's treatment. He was the father-in-law of the president of Ferrum Junior College. He was terminally ill and lived with the president. We drove about one mile on a gravel road to the president's home. This was a nice experience in that they were expecting me, and they were very appreciative of having nursing care for Grandpa during his last few days. He lived six days, and when he expired I called Dr. Green. He came to visit, showing respect for the family.

I had never before had the final say when a patient expired, yet Dr. Green came in the room and took a look, but did not check. Dr. Green didn't ask me, but told me that he had another patient for whom I was to care. I presented a bill, and they promptly gave me a check. I packed my belongings and loaded them in the truck. We had not driven very far when he told me that we would stop and see if one of his obstetrical cases was ready to deliver. We were detained for four hours. This was my first experience in a home delivery. A neighbor lady was there and had been with the mother during the birth of six other children. I do not know whether she considered herself a mid-wife or not. At least she had everything ready, according to Appalachia customs and circumstances. I told Dr. Green that I felt like a third party on an important date. The family knew that we were going to make a house call, another twelve miles on a mud road, and they invited us to eat the evening meal. They served dried beans and cornbread with fried apple pies. They were hospitable, friendly, and expressed appreciation for my being there with Dr. Green. This was a three-room house with a lean-to kitchen. We ate in the kitchen where it was drafty and cold. I shivered under my all-wool nurses' cape.

The February weather wasn't very kind to us. It was cold, and sleet formed a coating of ice on the windshield while we were caring for the mother and baby. In a very real sense, I wondered how we would make it, but I didn't make a comment. Darkness had settled in, and the road was narrow; the ruts muddy and deep. When we came to the lane that led to the house, less than a half-mile long, it was obvious that it would be very risky to try and navigate the steep terrain. Dr. Green had to get home that night and wanted to avoid sliding off the narrow mud road, which would require an all-night vigil. He had a pair of gum-boots that I wore over my shoes and a heavy coat that would fit over my nurses' cape. I carried my nurse's bag, and he carried my suitcase and his doctor bag. It was late when we got there, a dim light shone through the cracks of the wood shutters in the living room.

Dr. Green examined a sixty-four-year-old grandmother with double pneumonia. She was six days into the illness, and it was obvious she was a very sick person. Dr. Green left some medicine and asked me to get some food into her if I could. This was a one-room house with a dirt floor in the lean-to kitchen. A ladder attached to the side of the kitchen wall led to the sleeping facilities in the attic. It was midnight, but the daughter-law asked what I needed. I told her I wanted a large kettle of water to put on the hearth to heat for the patient's morning bath. I also needed a container for waste water and a container of cold water. I asked if they had some sheets for the bed. She said they could have some made by the morning. Neighbors had been sitting at night with the family, and my guess is they had a "sewing bee" in the kitchen during the rest of the night.

To say the least, the room was drafty. In fact, I asked if they could hang a comforter, of which they seemed to have plenty, over the shutter to keep the draft from my patient. The fireplace was large, and plenty of wood was stacked in the corner of the room which they replenished every morning. I kept a roaring fire night and day.

I had a very sick patient. She had been in bed six days with intermittent chills, high fever, and at times a subnormal low temperature. She had eaten very little and needed clean clothing and comforters. She spiked a fever at three o'clock in the morning. I gave her some cold water and her medicine and sponged her face and hands with tepid water.

She had not been bathed or had her clothing or the comforters changed since she had become sick. The first thing that I did was to get some food in her. She still had some temperature, but she recognized that I was taking care of her, though I am not sure she realized I had been there during the night. As soon as I heard someone in the kitchen, I asked for hot coffee and some cooked oatmeal. They were very prompt, and I succeeded in getting her to eat. I then asked for some clean comforters and the bed sheets, and I got both. The sheets were made of sugar sacks. I was very naive and had no suspicions about their livelihood.

On close inspection, I found that Grandma was wearing a suit of men's long underwear with hand-knitted, woolen, knee-high socks sewn to the underwear. The stitches were large and could be cut without damaging either. When I asked for clean underwear and socks they didn't have another pair of socks, but they agreed to wash the ones she had been wearing, and they brought clean underwear. I gave her a good bath, changed the comforters top and bottom, put sheets over the clean bottom comforter, and a sheet over her with two clean, heavy comforters on top. To make sure I did not chill her in the process, I used fruit jars of warm water inside a clean sugar sack on each part of her body that I exposed long enough to bathe. This process took most of the morning. Unfortunately, she spiked another temperature. I started a proctoclysis of tepid water through the rectum, not sure if this would bring down the temperature, but she was dehydrated and this was another way of getting fluid into her body. As the days passed, her temperature lessened, and I was successful in getting more food into her. On the fourth day, I got her up in the rocking chair in front of the open fire. Her socks had been washed and dried by that time, and they served as bed shoes. I fed her dinner as she sat in the rocking chair. I also combed and braided her hair, which made her feel better. She said, "My hair has not been combed since I've been sick." I put jars of hot water in her bed while she was sitting in the chair so the covers would be warm when the time came to return her to the bed. The rocking chair was a welcome change for her, and I was thrilled with the progress she was making. By the fifth day, she was fever-free. I was beginning to wonder when Dr. Green would come to see how we were getting along.

In all honesty, I was getting pretty weary myself. I had not been to bed for four nights. However, I slept in the rocking chair every night. I was dirty, and my uniform was filthy. I had worn a clean one when I came and brought a clean one with me, but two were in the laundry back in Ferrum which Dr. Green was to bring when he came. I was also getting rather hungry for some good food. After sizing up the situation, I decided I could live on hard boiled eggs and baked potatoes cooked on the hearth before the open fire. However, I did drink the coffee from the kitchen.

On the sixth day, Dr. Green came to find Grandma in the chair. After he read the chart he said, "I am going to take your nurse with me." As we got in the car, Dr. Green asked me if I had presented a bill. I was somewhat bewildered and said, "No, I didn't want to take bread out of the mouths of babes." He chided me a little, and I told him I had finally found out their livelihood. I would have felt guilty charging anything under the humble circumstance in that abode.

Dr. Green brought my laundry and took my dirty uniforms to be laundered. On the way to the next patient, he told me a little bit about the twenty-year-old young man with pneumonia. I was to do the same thing for this patient that I had done for Grandma. He complimented the chart and how I had managed her. I let him know that I was weary for a bath, clean clothes, and some sleep in a bed. Dr. Green said, "That will not be a problem where you are going this time." It was a three-room house with a functional kitchen. I told the mother that I had been on a case for five days and that I needed a little time to bathe and dress. The kitchen was fairly warm, and it was private. Dr. Green checked his patient and visited with the mother until I had refreshed myself. At least, I greeted my patient with a clean uniform and polished shoes. Dr. Green was pleased with the progress the young man had made in the three days since he had seen him.

I will call my patient "Jim." I inquired if he had been eating, the answer was not very much. I told him I wanted him to have plenty of fluids. His mother said he liked tomato juice, and while shaving off a week's growth of beard, I was able to get four ounces of tomato juice into him. Jim was in a half-sized bed in the living room. Jim also needed a good bath and a change of bed linens, which I decided to postpone until early morning. Jim was wearing pajamas and so I could massage his back and shoulders with rubbing alcohol. I brushed his hair and massaged his scalp thoroughly. I was able to get medicine and sassafras tea into him before bedtime. He was unable to eat the baked potato prepared by his mother for the evening meal, he ate a small amount of apple sauce. Since they had a cot in the kitchen, I asked them to bring it to the living room so I could get some sleep, if Jim slept. The mother seemed pleased to do this.

The mother was up early and had hot water on the kitchen range, and clean linens and pajamas all ready for the morning bath. I checked Jim's temperature, gave him his medicine with tomato juice, and fed him hot oatmeal for breakfast. For my breakfast, I ate fried home-canned apples, toast, and coffee. According to his mother, Jim had not had a bowel movement in four days. I gave him a tepid soapsuds enema, hoping that it would help take his temperature down, and got good results. By ten o'clock, Jim was in a clean bed, fed, bathed, and medicated; and I was hoping his temperature would go down without having to expose him to a cold spongebath in a room that was already drafty—the fireplace could not make the living room comfortable. However, by noon, Jim's temperature was down to normal. They also had a rocking chair with a heavy comforter that I used when I wasn't busy. I moved Jim's bed closer to the fire, and I kept a roaring fire going night and day.

I got the feeling that Jim and his mother lived in the kitchen more than in the living room, because the kitchen stove kept the kitchen more comfortable than the fireplace kept the living room. The weather was cold, with lots of wind and snow.

Four days passed before Dr. Green came by. By that time, Jim had had one day without fever. He was weak, eating sparingly, and had spent some time propped up in bed; but he had not made it to the rocking chair. Dr. Green checked him and felt that I could be dismissed. I presented a bill and was paid in cash. I packed my things and put them in the back of the truck. I could not wait to tell Dr. Green how much I had enjoyed nursing Jim and visiting with his mother. Their house was a typical Appalachian house, subtly refined. Jim's mother had a garden and preserved food. She had a variety of canned goods that seemed quite adequate. Though bed sheets were made from sugar sacks, that did not mean that Jim was in the business of operating a still. Sugar sacks were cheap and could be bought from people who operated stills, an apparatus for distilling alcoholic liquors.

When we left, the sun was shining, but the snow was frozen on the road, and Dr. Green drove with caution. He finally told me we would be stopping to "catch" another baby. This was a young mother and it was her first baby. Though I was on my own in getting things ready for this delivery. I had observed the other experience, and I had no trouble, except that she had no rubber sheets. However, I had a small one that I had used in giving enemas. She had been in labor for several hours with hard contractions, I immediately started timing her contractions, and after an hour, I told her that she needed to get into bed. Because I wanted to see if she was capping with the contractions—she was. She was almost exhausted, and the contractions were three to four minutes apart. I reported this to Dr. Green, and he came to check. He reached down into his bag and handed me an inhalant of ether vapor, and told me to administer it when he told me to. Within the hour, we had a baby. Dr. Green told me as soon as I had finished with the mother and baby, we could be home by dark. That was music to my ears. I knew that I would be staying at the home of the Ferrum College's president.

I bathed and dressed the baby, changed the mother's bed, and dressed her wounded bottom, and massaged her stomach until the uterus shrank in size. Dr. Green came in and gave the mother some advice about caring for the baby and herself. I packed up, and we were off to chug along the cold, rutted, snow-covered roads for about twenty miles. We missed dinner. Dr. Green called and told them that I would be in sometime between dark and bedtime. They had saved me some food, which was delicious. I also spent a little time cleaning out my nursing bag and suitcase. But the divine moment came when I immersed myself in a top of hot water that seemed like heaven on earth. I then got a good night's sleep. I had forgotten what a good bed was like!

The next morning, the doorbell rang, and a grandson of Grandma, my first case, left the exact amount of money for the five days that I had nursed his grandma. When I told Dr. Green, he said, "I know for sure the family has $15,000 in the Ferrum bank." I have never felt so humble in all my life.

Several times during my stay of six weeks with Dr. Green in the heart of Appalachia, I remembered the words of the graduate nurse: "One's nursing training is never over until she has served a term with Dr. Green in the Blue Ridge Mountains." No truer words have ever been uttered.

In 1939, I graduated in Nursing from Roanoke General Hospital, Roanoke, Virginia.

Chapter Seven

Romance and Marriage

Having been in school five years beyond high school, I passed my state board for registered nurse (R.N.), which carried a high degree of successful employment with a variety of specialties from which to choose. I had worked as a supervisor in the hospital where I trained. I had a learning experience nursing for Dr. Green during February in the Blue Ridge Mountains of Virginia deep within Appalachia. I felt it was time for me to clear the deck, to reflect on where I had been and where I was going.

On the occasion of the Church of the Brethren's Annual Conference in June 1940, I went with Daddy to Ocean Grove, New Jersey, for a diversion and change of scenery. The outcome of this vacation changed my life forever. Little did I recognize when the meeting was over, the innermost pride and joy for a young man who, from all indications, knew who he was, what he was doing, and where he was going, and who would some day be mine forever.

I attended the program for young adults and Elgin was there, and after the program he came over and introduced himself and asked if I would have dinner with him in the evenings. I accepted. For the rest of the week, both families were aware that we were spending time together. However, when Daddy, Uncle John, John Junior, and I spent the afternoon at the beach, Elgin had something else planned.

At the time, I wondered what could be more enjoyable than an afternoon on the Atlantic Coast—and I am still wondering! I can't remember when we got back together, but when we did I told Elgin the water was warm, the sand was white and shiny, and was my first experience in beachcombing. My Daddy in a bathing suit with his white hair and beard looked liked Moses come to life. Uncle John was the only one who braved the deep water as John Junior occupied himself taking pictures.

I'm afraid I didn't absorb much knowledge or information from the conference; but I was excited to be there, and the time to part came all too soon. The night before both families were to leave for New York to see the sights and visit the World's Fair, Elgin's good night kiss unmistakably confirmed that a spark had been ignited.

The next day, Daddy and I went to the Empire State Building. Elgin and his family visited later and found our names on the register. We spent three days at the New York's World Fair. But before Daddy and I left the city, I wanted to visit Saks Fifth Avenue. Ladies' ready-to-wear was on the third floor. We took the elevator and were greeted by a saleswoman wanting to know what she could show us. Daddy replied, "Madam, if you will not charge me for sitting in this chair, I beg to be excused." I told her I wanted a tam. She led me to a room showcasing a variety of women's head dressings. I selected a large, white, corded-silk tam pleated into a black velvet band that adjusted depending on whether you wore it low or high on your forehead. Since this transaction didn't take very long, I returned to the elevators and collected Daddy; and we went back to our tourist accommodation. We were tired—in fact exhausted. I took a long soak in the bathtub, bandaged my blistered feet, and went to bed. I've forgotten the details of how and where we met our ride for home the next morning. I do remember that they stopped long enough to drop me off where I lived, in Roanoke, Virginia. If I remember correctly, a card and a letter from Elgin was waiting for me when I arrived home and I spent some time reflecting on my first vacation. I had never been to an Annual Conference, I had never been to New York City, and I had never met a handsome young man: business-like, polite, and caring, but one thing for sure—given the opportunity, I would immediately say "Yes." We established a daily correspondence that led to Elgin's visiting me in Roanoke in the spring of 1941.

But for now, I was on my own, paying my own bills with confidence. When I got back to Roanoke, I put my name on the register and returned to private duty.

I was on a night case when Elgin arrived. We took the better part of two days for him to get acquainted with Uncle Roy and Aunt Hazel, Betty Lee, and Jean Poff. He toured the hospital and met some of the staff as well as some of the girls who graduated in my class. He also met my landlady and her daughter Virginia. Elgin spent the night with Uncle Roy and left the next afternoon before I went to work. Elgin came on the bus but hitchhiked back to North Manchester, Indiana. I got a letter telling me that he had slept in a hay field the first night but arrived home the next day.

I was discharged from my case the morning after Elgin left. I was called to take a surgical case, seven to three shift and asked to take my patient home when she had recuperated enough from a broken hip to make the trip. The lady, who lived in Waynesboro, Virginia, was past middle-age and still mad at herself for falling on soapsuds that had drained off the porch while scrubbing the floor. She was a fun person to be with and a good patient. Her husband was the superintendent of schools and depended on Bridgewater College for a supply of well-prepared teachers. He seemed pleasantly surprised when he learned that I had attended Bridgewater for two years.

Elgin called me several times while I was there, and they also were aware that I was often writing letters. The wall telephone didn't allow for much privacy. From the beginning, they answered the phone and knew it was a man's voice. Different members of the family questioned me about the phone calls and my frequent letter writing, but I didn't offer too much information.

In three weeks, my patient was walking with help. The family was to be the judge as to how long they needed help. The Blue Ridge Parkway had just opened, and they wanted me to go with them for a week's trip along the Skyline Drive and the Parkway. This was lots of fun and I almost felt guilty taking pay for her care. Incidentally, her ability to walk with confidence improved immeasurably. She enjoyed the change from the daily routine and the scenic beauty along the way and so did I. After we returned to her home, I took the bus back to Roanoke.

I continued to work, but Elgin and I made plans that I would visit his folks before the summer was over. One afternoon, after leaving work, I boarded a Greyhound bus, taking the West Virginia route to North Manchester, Indiana. It was rough sleeping as the driver navigated the hairpin curves of the West Virginia mountains. Elgin met me the next day at Fort Wayne about mid-morning.

Elgin's home was adjacent to the college campus. I was impressed with the blooming flowers, garden, and plum orchard. Dad Kintner was a horticulturist of renown, and Mother Kintner had won lots of ribbons at flower shows. Elgin was part of a large family, second from the bottom of eight children—seven boys and one girl. Elgin's father was a science teacher at Manchester College. His mother was a housewife and an excellent cook, with lots of interest in the community, church work, and, especially, the College Women's Club. In the few days that I spent there, I met all of the family, including Ruth, the only girl, who lived in Lansing, Michigan. It took me a while to get them placed in their rightful abodes, and properly labeled into their varied professional callings in the health field. From the top down: Galen, an optometrist; Dana, a dentist; Ruth, a dietitian; Kenneth, an optometrist; Quentin, a general practitioner; Burton, a general practitioner; Elgin, a pathologist; and Bob, an anesthesiologist.

When I came back from visiting Elgin's folks, I was called for another hospital case, three to eleven shift. I liked this shift because I had some time during the day to call my own. Sometimes, however, when all the other private duty nurses were busy, I took my turn working two eight-hour shifts. This happened to me on the three to eleven shift. In a very few days, I was also working the seven to three shift.

As I drifted between working, writing letters, and sleeping, I felt that the next step in our romance would be to invite Elgin down to meet my family. Plans were made. I removed my name from the register and went home, Elgin came down.

When Mother met Elgin for the first time, she said, "Ethel, somebody wasted beauty on that boy." After dinner, Elgin and I took a walk to the pine forest overlooking a valley and the Great Smoky Mountains. Elgin was fascinated with the sights and sounds at eventide, and I felt so carefree and happy! The next day, Daddy felt that we should take a swing around Cades Cove and Clingman's Dome in the Great Smoky Mountain National Park, and we did.

One day, we took a walk to the church, sat in the cemetery, and savored a view seen by too few people—blue sky, green grass, and flat valley surrounding the four-mile-wide Douglas Lake that reflected the Great Smoky Mountain. Elgin must have thought this to be the perfect place to propose to me, and he did. I was thrilled and speechless for at least a second. I accepted. He gave me his Phi Kappa Rho key, which I cherished very much. But I suddenly wondered how we would manage to coordinate everything.

Elgin had a few words with Daddy about our engagement, and I was told they had a very pleasant conversation. However, Daddy was a little concerned about Elgin being a sophomore with two more years to finish medical school. Elgin had a part-time job at the Industrial Clinic in Indianapolis, Indiana. One thing for sure; we were not going to have a long engagement.

We decided that I would move to Indianapolis, apply for a job at Methodist Hospital (the largest private hospital in the United States), find a place to live, and then decide how soon we could afford to get married.

One afternoon, Elgin told me he wanted to take a bath. I pointed to the summer house. The tub, towels, washcloth, and soap were down there. I said, "You know how to get rain water out of the cistern, and I will put a pail of hot water on the back porch."

Mother and I were in the kitchen cooking dinner. When Elgin finished, he flung the door wide open, planted his bare feet firmly in the doorway, and called out, "What must I do with the water?"

I yelled out the window, "Strain it and pour it back into the cistern." I didn't get a reply, but I saw Elgin behind the summer house emptying the galvanized tub. We all had a good laugh, and it was hard to tell who was kidding whom.

August 7, 1941, Elgin went home to North Manchester from Indianapolis, picked up his folks' car, and came down to Roanoke, Virginia, to move to Indianapolis. He got the promise of a room for me in a rooming house about two blocks from the hospital before he came down. The thing that I dreaded most was taking Indiana's state board. Reciprocity became the order of the day in less than one year.

However the hospital hired me immediately and put me on the orthopedic ward in the basement. There were many unfortunate results of industrial accidents such as broken bones, casts, and Bradford frames, and amid rampant smoke fumes, tobacco expectorate which filled the emeses basins around the clock. Many patients in body casts were hooked up to pulleys that allowed some freedom in moving the body around, and traction maintained the proper alignment of a set fracture. Casts, shoulder slings, and braces were the rule of the orthopedic floor, not the exception. I didn't allow myself to think that I wouldn't like this floor because *beggars can't be choosers.*

It wasn't long until Bertha Pullen, Superintendent of Nurses, asked if I would supervise the surgical floor. By this time I had passed the Indiana nursing boards. She raised my salary $20 a month and provided an assistant supervisor to support my efforts. This was a real challenge in that the bed capacity was fifty patients and it was unusual to have a vacant bed. Before the days of recovery rooms, the patients were brought directly from the surgical stretcher to the floor. It was not unusual to have eight or ten surgical patients a day. Back then, surgical patients were kept in the hospital for eight to ten days. What surprised me the most was that I got day duty on both assignments.

After I became acclimated to the surgical floor, I felt that we had made progress toward our life together. Elgin had finished another year of medical school, and we thought it would be nice to have an early spring wedding in 1942. I'm not sure how we came up with April 4, but I was concerned about the weather. I wanted it to be a nice arm spring day—and it was.

It was nice that Elgin, Burton, and Quentin (the three little ones) could be in medical school on the Indiana University campus at the same time. It was not often we could be together, but when we did it was fun. I got to know Burton's girlfriend, Ellen Jane, and we became close friends. Ellen Jane often spent the night with me when Elgin worked nights at the Industrial Clinic. Quentin met Christine Carlson three days before the spring prom. Arriving at the prom, I was known among close friends as Elgin's girl from south of the line, the heart of Appalachia, which created a few remarks like, "Elgin, she's got on shoes." I don't know how Elgin managed all the in-fun cultural slurs, but I readily confessed, and when I felt it necessary, I defended my culture and upbringing with fun and pride. We had a wonderful evening and enjoyed Christine ever so much.

Soon after midnight, we went to our respective abodes. At three o'clock in the morning Quentin called me to talk about his Christine. He said they were going to get married. I told him there was nothing wrong with his marrying Christine, but for heaven's sake why wasn't he asleep at that time in the morning? Quentin wanted to talk until daylight about his love and affection for Christine. I told him he needed to call Christine and tell her what he was telling me: "Good night, Quentin."

Christine and Quentin knew that Elgin and I had our date set for April 4, 1942, but they got married one month to the day before our wedding date. This incident created a conversation piece for both families. When asked, they explained, they had to find a time when Dad Kintner was free to 'tie the knot'. Dad Kintner tied the knot for seven of the eight children.

As Elgin and I worked on the details of our wedding, bit by bit things fell into place. I went home two weeks before the wedding. The wedding was announced in the three churches in the Oak Grove community and an invitation was put in the churches' bulletins. We sent hand-written invitations, with Elgin's Phi Kappa Rho insignia, to special friends.

Ethel May Montgomery, one of my friends from Bridgewater, came down to play the organ. The background of the stage was decorated with rhododendron, and baskets of white gladioli were on either side of the stage.

Mother and Dad Kintner and little Bob stayed at our house, but Daddy got rooms at Morristown Hotel for Burton, Ellen Jane, Elgin, Ethel May, and me. I went home to dress, and the others went to church directly from the hotel. Daddy escorted me. My sister Erlene was maid of honor, and Burton served as Elgin's best man. Dad Kintner said the ceremony, and the reception was held at Shepherd Inn in Dandridge.

After the wedding we went home, undressed, and packed our gifts in barrels to be shipped to us. Dressed in our traveling clothes, we ate dinner, and my sister Evelyn and her husband, A.B. Watkins, drove us to Knoxville. The bad boys tied old tin buckets and wash pans under the car, and they made so much noise we had to stop and remove them. We spent the night in the Farragut Hotel and the next day we took a bus to Indianapolis and our apartment.

A few weeks before I left for the wedding, we had rented an unfurnished efficiency apartment across the street from Methodist Hospital. We furnished it with slightly damaged furniture from the railroad station though we did buy a new living room couch and a floor lamp. It was so nice to have our own apartment to which to come home. I appreciated living close to the hospital where I worked.

Elgin was in his senior year of medical school and his work was very demanding. He was beginning to experience clinical treatment and observation of patients. I had adjusted to my work schedule, even though the United States was involved in World War II, which created problems for society in general. The bombing of Pearl Harbor by Japan on December 7, 1941, came as a real surprise, and not a single person escaped the degradation of this militant act. The hospital suffered from a deficit of hospital personnel, which made a demanding job more difficult. Many nurses left to be with their husbands in boot camp.

During the fall holidays of 1942, I began to lose my breakfast with little or no warning. We soon learned that I was pregnant, and that the "d-date" would be about the time Elgin graduated from medical school in June. I resigned my job two months before our baby was due. I had been able to wear my uniforms only with the aid of safety pins and the bottom of a white undershirt to hide my bulging stomach.

In the wake of the exitement Miss Pullen, superintendent of nurses, lost her instructor for "Fundamentals of Nursing." She asked me if I would finish the term. I told her about my uniform problem and that at this stage of my pregnancy I didn't want to buy maternity garments. She replied, "You can wear anything you want to or nothing at all, if you will finish the term for the beginning students." I agreed to try. The class met from nine to ten-forty-five three days a week. Elgin got a teaching job in a private boys' school to finish the year for the same reason that I finished the term for the nurses—the teacher was drafted.

I was concerned about Elgin's military service. The draft board in Wabash County, his legal residence, wanted to draft him before he graduated, even though the law was clear that medical students were to be deferred until after graduation. Elgin wanted to join the United States Public Health Service and go on active duty after graduation. He appeared before an attorney representing the draft board and shortly was commissioned in the USPHS.

We were stationed at the United States Marine Public Health Hospital at Windmill Point, near Detroit, Michigan. Elgin completed his internship and went on regular staff duty with officer's pay, which was wonderful.

We lived in an upstairs apartment about a mile from the hospital. I was thrilled to have a baby for whom to care instead of the patients in the hospital beds. Beccie entered this world cooing; she skipped the crawling stage, but she cruised her bed and playpen a hundred times a day. At nine months, Beccie was walking and she was verbal, although to us it was meaningless jargon, but not for long. She was beginning to get a few sprigs of hair, with which I was thrilled. We celebrated her first birthday on June 9, 1944, on the small stoop leading from the second-floor living room, which was still covered with snow at the end of May.

On occasional winter afternoons I would skate on the frozen canal and pull Beccie on the sled to meet Elgin at the hospital. In the spring and early fall, I would bicycle to meet Elgin with Beccie in the rumble seat. I enjoyed dressing Beccie in her finest, riding the trolley downtown, and crossing the Detroit River in a ferry boat to Windsor, Canada. It was a lot of fun window shopping and having lunch at my favorite tea room.

My most frightening experience with Beccie was when she fell down twenty uncarpeted steps to the landing on the first floor in our apartment building. By the time I got her cleaned up and her wounds dressed, she was calm, but I was still shaking. A tooth cut her lower lip and she had a bruise on her forehead, plus a small cut on one finger.

A place for Beccie to play was a problem, because I couldn't let her out alone, and so I spent a lot of time with other officers' wives who had children Beccie's age on the beaches of the Detroit River and Lake St. Clare.

During the three years we lived in Detroit, we had a "Victory Garden" on a plot of ground between the hospital and where we lived. We enjoyed the vegetables, but the growing season was very short. It wasn't unusual to have a cool weather in September, frost in October, followed by a hard freeze in November, and snow that turned to ice that covered both the front and back stoops for the winter.

We were very fortunate in that Dr. Geyer kept Elgin's name out of Washington and Elgin spent three years in the Public Health Service at the United States Marine Hospital in Detroit. The war was over on August 14, 1945, but Elgin served one more year before he was discharged. Elgin had a year's excellent training in surgery which qualified him for a surgery residency. However, when Elgin was a free man again, all of the surgical residencies had been taken. His better judgment led him to set up in practice in Goshen, Indiana. I was thrilled to be settled in a new house in a new subdivision. Beccie had lots of playmates and she could safely be outside by herself or with other children.

Goshen was a town of twenty-thousand people. Goshen College, a cabinet factory, and other small businesses were surrounded by progressive farmland noted for high yields in corn, soybeans, and silage. The land was flat, and the soil was rich.

The medical community welcomed Elgin warmly, and he wasted no time in securing and furnishing an office on the top floor of the Shoot's Building. Elgin's bronze "shingle" was on a bulletin board adjacent to the entrance of the building. Richard, our only son, cherishes his Daddy's signboard very much.

We attended the Church of the Brethren, made friends in the community, and visited Dana, who lived in South Bend; Kenneth who lived in Mishawaka; and Burton, who lived in Elkhart. On weekends we would often drive to North Manchester to visit Dad and Mother Kintner. After the war, Quentin, Dana, and Galen settled on the West Coast.

Mother Kintner was great on having family get-togethers and we have pictures representing marriages, graduations, anniversaries, and grandchildren over a period of thirty years. Mother's favorite expression, when people asked her how many grandchildren she had was, "Twenty at the last count."

Before long I was involved with the medical auxiliary and was a member of Psi Iota Xi Sorority, which did community work with proceeds going to the hospital planning board. Elgin and I were involved socially and professionally in the community, medical society, women's auxiliary, and the hospital, which inspired our maternal instinct for more family.

We had so thoroughly enjoyed Beccie that we wanted more children. I had been to a specialist to see why I wasn't getting pregnant. Our gynecologist told me that he didn't know why we had a fertility problem, but it was not impossible for us to get pregnant, but rather improbable. We decided to acquire the rest of our family by adoption. We were investigated by a social worker and she was somewhat bothered because we didn't have a three-bedroom house. I didn't bother to express my attitude about wealth and possessions versus love and care of a child. She did, however, explain the rules governing adoptions: adoptive parents had to be in residence for two years and be visited periodically by the agency before they could be recommended for a baby.

Elgin's practice was keeping him comfortably busy. His obstetrical practice was of great concern, both before the birth and afterwards. However the pediatric part of his practice was frustrating, in that a small child can get sick with a high fever, be unresponsive, drift in and out of awareness, and nothing can be found diagnostically. This situation created anxiety for the parents and the doctor. Night calls got to be nightmares for Elgin. He was very conscientious about his practice of medicine, but he wanted his practice to be more satisfying and less frustrating. Unbeknownst to me, Elgin had written a letter to Dr. Harold Gorden inquiring about resident training in pathology. Elgin called from the office and said, "Go downstairs to my desk and find the letter from Dr. Gorden, and read it to me." This letter was in invitation for Elgin to enter the resident program through the Veterans Administration in Louisville, Kentucky. I was stunned but not too surprised.

Our eighteen months in Goshen was very enjoyable, especially for Beccie and me. Elgin had talked his problem over with Dr. Girodona, the pathologist who directed the Goshen laboratory, and he encouraged Elgin to go into pathology and become certified in both clinical and anatomical pathology. This change took us to the Veterans Hospital in Louisville, Kentucky.

Here I am, modeling the tam purchased at Saks Fifth Avenue in New York City, one year before I was married.

Our wedding photo, taken April 4, 1942, at the French Broad Church of the Brethren, White Pine, Tennessee.

Elgin and I with our first child, Beccie.

Chapter Eight

Change in Plans

In the last fifty years, the image of change has been reflected in people and how they access their own abilities, strengths, growth, and maturity. This often leads to a career change or more training in one's own calling.

Elgin, in his educational and professional development, had the opportunity to evaluate negative and positive feedback and see how the two processes interplayed in relation to his own development, understanding, needs, and with his scientific and research abilities. Whatever Elgin's motivation for changing from general practice to pathology, it was not misdirected. I believe Elgin's record in laboratory medicine indicates that he sought new levels of excellence, achieving high standards and real accountability in practice.

Elgin and I agreed to sell the house and Elgin's practice. We moved from Goshen to Louisville, Kentucky, on July 1, 1948, so Elgin could complete two years of resident training in Pathologic Anatomy. We would then move to South Bend, Indiana, so he could attend the South Bend Medical Foundation for one year of Clinical Pathology, necessary to become board certified.

Knowing that we would be living on a very tight budget for three years, we went shopping. Elgin bought a suit and a top coat. I bought a suit, and we got Beccie her first store bought "snow suit." It was a two-piece suit, medium weight, for a more moderate climate. The jacket was suitable for school.

Upon investigation, we learned that Louisville's housing department was building three city blocks of apartments which would contain two-bedroom family units. We got an end apartment, ground level, perpendicular to the driveway, with all four units finished. We liked this location because we were least disturbed by the noise of the machinery and the builders. One afternoon I observed that the workers built a bon-fire with the blocks accumulated from the day's finishing of door facings and trim in the apartments. I asked if I could have some blocks with which my daughter could play. "You can have all you want," came the reply. Beccie was thrilled that I retrieved and put in her bedroom an assortment of sizes and shapes to be sorted and stacked as she saw fit.

Moving out of the state before we become certified by the adoption agency for a baby was discouraging indeed. However, our feasibility study had been completed, and we had talked with our attorney, Dick Mehl, about our plans. He understood the problems created when moving from one state to another and promised his support and help if fortune came his way.

I felt that moving from Goshen was almost over when we got the van packed and on its way. We were ready to leave, and the truck was to be there before the van arrived. We stopped over the noon hour and ate in a hurry, but Elgin went to the rest room and stayed an awful long time. He had worn a mustache as long as we had been married, and he decided to appear at Veterans Hospital clean-shaven. When he came out of the rest room, I noticed that he carefully put something in the trunk of the car. I didn't ask any questions, and didn't expect any wrongdoing, but I didn't notice anything different. We did arrive before the van, so we stopped at the grocery store to make sure we wouldn't starve or be away when the van eventually drove up. We were unloading the van after dark, and the only thing that got put in place were our beds. Beccie was more than ready for bed, and so were we. When I stopped long enough to admit that our day reminded me that things would be different for us for a while, that was the first time I noticed Elgin's clean-shaven upper lip. He seemed a little relieved that he wouldn't have to tell me.

After getting the apartment fixed up, meeting some of our neighbors, becoming acquainted with the neighborhood, visiting the school Beccie would attend, and being asked by one of our neighbors to attend the Presbyterian Church where she sang in the choir, I felt a little more worthwhile.

We did attend the Presbyterian Church downtown. The minister was Reverend Gilmore, the brother of Reverend Leland Gilmore, who lived in Maryville. Reverend Gilmore visited us and made us feel welcome. We told him we were impressed with the new curriculum materials, "Christian Faith and Life." Fortunately or unfortunately as the case might be, the famous cafeteria, "The Blue Boar," across the street, was as tempting as the food was delicious. We succumbed almost every Sunday as did most of the congregation.

We were pretty much settled in the apartment and the community and Elgin was accustomed to his routine, when he announced that we could go up home for the week-end! Unbeknownst to us Dick Mehl had called Burton (Elgin's physician brother) and told him he had a nice eight-month-old baby boy available for placement. Burton knew that we were on our way up and surprised us with the good news. Burton and Elgin went over to talk to Dick and see the baby. They were impressed. It was hard for Yi and me to function in the kitchen with such exciting news. Yi, as usual, had a wonderful meal; we enjoyed eating and talking about our new baby, Richard, whom we had named after Dick Mehl. I'm not sure who suggested the name Richard, but we were calling him by that name before we were sure we could take him back with us. Since Star and Beccie were upstairs playing, they didn't get the good news until the next day.

Elgin and I went on Sunday together to see Richard. It was truly love at first sight. Dick said, "You can take him today if you want to." We left Dick's office with a beautiful baby boy. We were on route to Grandma and Grandpa Kintner's to spend the night, and they were surprised, but pleased, when we walked in with a new baby. Mother exclaimed, "Where did he come from." We told her it happened by chance! Later in the year we would need to go back to Elkhart to appear before the judge to finalize the adoption procedure.

When we got home to Louisville the next day, we had Richard with us. The families in our complex were shocked and pleased. I let all three neighbors know about Richard before we went to bed. Beccie and Richard were the only children in our unit, so Beccie was very attentive to him. In fact, she cautiously shared her favorite doll, "Sparkle Plenty," with him.

The next day Elgin came home early, and he and Beccie took care of Richard while I went shopping for clothes. When Beccie came home from school, I would let Richard play in the play pen, and Beccie would sit on the steps and watch him. Beccie liked to take him out of the play pen and have him sit with her on the steps. Beccie saw him take his first step, and she screamed for me to come and look! Richard enriched our lives and the lives of the extended families.

The church nursery was a little shocked when Beccie and I walked in and announced that this was Beccie's little brother. One Sunday after church, a number of people were headed for the Blue Boar for lunch, and a tall, elegantly dressed man, swinging a briefcase, was walking toward us. Richard threaded through his legs and kept walking. The man stamped, stuttered, flailed his arms, stepped aside, and we all passed him by. Afterwards, I felt a little guilty that I didn't stop and confess that had been my son, and apologize that he had been so aggressive.

When an apartment became available on the base we moved. There were other children of hospital personnel who lived in the barracks. Swimming became a daily function, and Beccie and Richard didn't lack for birthday parties and other social functions. In the fall Beccie started school, and she had other friends to walk with her to and from school. We lived upstairs, but it was safe for Richard to play in the playground and we can't remember when he couldn't swim. He startled many adults by swimming the length of the pool when he was two years old.

Elgin was enjoying his studies, and I was enjoying Beccie, a first-grader and Richard, a little toddler. Then I told Elgin, "I have to have one more baby; I will, beg, borrow, or steal if necessary." Time passed, and one day Burton called and told us that he would have a baby that was going to be put up for adoption. After some investigation, we let Burton know that we were interested. I wanted to keep it a secret from Beccie and Richard until close to the time for the baby to be born. However, from six months on I marked the calendar days with an X.

Elgin seemed relaxed during his "back to school experience." He enjoyed being free when off duty. It must have been a relief knowing that he would not do house calls, deliver babies, be on call, or have to respond to phone calls in the middle of the night. However, in the latter part of his last year of pathology training, he became anxious about finding a hospital that needed a pathologist trained in both clinical and anatomical pathology. Elgin had put out feelers and visited several hospitals in Michigan and Indiana, but for various reasons nothing developed. When Elgin was out investigating leads, he always called home. A bulletin finally came listing hospitals needing pathologists, and Maryville, Tennessee, was listed. Of course Elgin didn't know anything about the Maryville-Alcoa community. I answered all his questions, of which there were many. He must have been impressed because he got home late that same night.

Elgin called in response to the Blount Memorial Hospital's inquiry about a pathologist, and we were invited down to see the hospital and community. It seemed that Dr. Lee and Grace Callaway were in charge of the afternoon and evening get together. Several staff members and wives gathered for dinner at the Chilhowee Inn in Townsend, Tennessee. Elgin was impressed with the hospital and the staff in particular. The evening was punctuated with hospitality, good food, and a warm friendliness that led Elgin to believe they in fact, did need a full-time pathologist qualified in both clinical and anatomical laboratory medicine. They mentioned the attributes in the Maryville-Alcoa-Blount County community that made living there worthwhile, and on a lighter note was Dr. Lee Callaway telling some of his prize-winning jokes.

We left feeling good about the prospects of this being a mutually beneficial situation, but no commitment was made, and we were left wondering. In a few days we got a letter inviting us back to talk about a contract.

Elgin responded promptly, but told them I couldn't come—we had a new baby. Unfortunately, Johanna was born at seven months. Burton had a pediatrician check her, and we were told that she was a strong, four-pound, premature baby, but she had lost six ounces. This news was very depressing, and Elgin and I told Burton to keep us posted, that we wanted to do for her what ever needed to be done.

Elgin went by himself to Blount Memorial Hospital and came back with a contract. Incidentally, I believe he told some of the staff about our new, premature baby. Although Elgin had a few more working days with the

South Bend Medical Foundation, nevertheless, we were making plans to move to Maryville, Tennessee. We were getting information every day about Johanna, and we felt it best to get settled in Tennessee, then I would fly back and pick her up when she was discharged.

One day Burton got a nasty surprise. He was told that an outburst of impetigo in the hospital nursery was forcing a complete evacuation. Burton called and told us. Johanna was a strong and healthy but premature baby, and she had not gained back her birth weight. Burton met us at the hospital, and we got Johanna and went to Burton's house for dinner. Yi, on short notice, as usual, still had a good dinner. Burton and Yi felt like we were leaving with their baby, and Elgin and I could understand why.

When I left the hospital with Johanna, I was given a few instructions about how to care for a premature infant. It is best to use sterile gauze for diapers, and premature-size nipples; to feed on demand; and if she slept longer than two hours in the daytime, awake and feed her. Johanna was not to be handled any more than necessary for feeding and bathing.

At ten o'clock one evening I was feeding Johanna, and Elgin said, "I am going to be up late and I will take care of her until I go to bed, then you can finish the night." The next morning I woke up and said to Elgin, "Did you feed Johanna?" He said, "No," and in the same breath, "Ethel, did you feed Johanna?" I said, "No." We were afraid to look in the bassinet, but we did. She was squirming and trying real hard to squeeze a tear. From then on, we fed her late in the evening, and didn't feed her at night unless she woke up, which was not often.

The next day, Bob's brother (then a teenager) called to tell us that he had been to hear Mario Lanza, a popular tenor of the day, and he wanted us to hear him too. I promptly responded, "Bob I can't leave Johanna." Bob replied, "I am going to come and keep her for you." I worried a little, but I did have confidence that Bob would be more reliable than anybody else. In fact, I wouldn't have known about Mario Lanza being in South Bend had it not been for Bob. When Bob came, I didn't know what he was expecting to see, but he was as poised as if he specialized in taking care of premature babies. I instructed him about the diaper change, and when she woke up, to feed her. She was on a small blanket and the gauze diaper was in place. If she needed a clean diaper, he should put the soiled one in a paper bag and get a clean one out of the box. If he fed her, he should take the blanket with the diaper in place and hold her in his arms. He was to get as much down her as he could, but if she fell asleep, he should put her back in the bassinet. Somehow, to this day Johanna and Richard have more Kintner uncles showing a little more favoritism to them than to the other two siblings.

Elgin came home about the time we usually eat and told me that the van would come in morning and pack our household furniture. I had asked our landlady, who lived upstairs, if she would take care of Johanna for us the day that we packed the van. She seemed pleased to be asked.

We were to take only the necessities. We were paying by the pound. The kitchen stove didn't qualify, but the pool table with six inches of slate had to go. However, it is still in the family and it was an antique to begin with. We didn't have a house in Maryville, and the furniture was in storage. Elgin was staying in the hotel, and I was at my parents' home with the children. One evening I was feeding Johanna, and Mother asked if she could hold her for a few minutes. Mother said, "Ethel, when Johanna gets a few years old, it would be so nice to have another baby." In less than a month I was back reporting that I was pregnant. I told Mother that this one would be her baby, and I was going to call it Ella even if it was a boy!

Richard Charles Kintner, born March 2, 1948, Elkhart, Indiana.

Johanna Kintner, born May 24, 1951, Elkhart, Indiana.

Chapter Nine

Dreams Come True

Dreams mean different things to different people, but for me it meant the end of moving around and the beginning of a settled life in a community where the children would have adequate opportunities—culturally, religiously, and educationally.

Elgin was to practice medicine as a pathologist, his choice of medical specialty, at the Blount Memorial Hospital. I felt privileged to create a happy home for our family of five and be pregnant.

Elgin became discouraged in finding a house for us to rent or buy and had resigned himself to finding something temporary. A new duplex on the corner of Mountain View and Cunningham Street was small for a family of five, but he thought it worth investigation. Elgin happened to stop by when Mrs. Ova Lindsey, the owner, came by to inspect the day's work. She seemed thrilled to rent, but reminded us that workmen would be around finishing the other side of the duplex and also converting a garage into a dwelling.

Elgin had the furniture moved out of storage and into the house before he came up to get us. He came Saturday afternoon and described in detail where we would be living, but was quick to add that we would still look for a house.

I can't begin to describe my feelings of joy as we drove to Maryville Sunday afternoon. We had been scattered, and now we would be settled. We had an only child for five years, but now we had three children, and I was pregnant. In the past, our housing had been modest, but now we could have a house that would accommodate a family of six with comfort. We would find one!

We got to Maryville in time to make the beds before we "lay me down to sleep." Our duplex faced Oak Park and the two sets of double windows in the living room required window dressings. The next day I bought a bolt of burlap and as time permitted, I made pull drapes for the windows. We bought a rug for the living room floor. Bit by bit, I got things in place, but knowing this arrangement was temporary, I didn't do unnecessary furnishings or decorating. With our dining room furniture in one end of the living room, things seemed a little crowded, at best. We had two bedrooms and bath upstairs. Beccie and Richard shared the same bedroom until Ella came along and shared our bedroom, then Johanna moved over with Beccie, and Richard moved to the attic. We used the attic for storage, but by moving everything to the back and under the rafters and putting in a partition, we created enough room for Richard's bed at the head of the stairs. At least he had cross ventilation with windows at either end. In fact, he liked his sleeping quarters.

Mr. Cam Anderson, a real estate agent, a native of Dandridge, Tennessee, and a friend to the family had read the write-up in the paper about a new doctor and his family moving to town and called to welcome me. I told him we were in need of a house, and he assured me he could find one.

I explained to Cam our need for a three-bedroom house with at least a bath-and-a-half, but preferably two baths. Cam and I spent a lot of time looking for a house that would meet our needs. This was in July of 1951, and at that time, a house could not be found with the room we needed that didn't have to be completely renovated, remodeled, and decorated. In desperation I asked Cam if he could find a three-bedroom house with a bath and a path. (I'm not sure he appreciated the remark.) However, he called the next morning and asked if I would look at one more house. It was several miles down Montvale Road. Cam walked me through the house, down the hall, through the kitchen, onto the back porch, and out to the garden plot, where he picked up a clod of red clay and ground it to a find dust, saying, "Ethel this is the finest of Tennessee red loam." With this display of Appalachian culture which we both knew so well, we gave up on house hunting.

In 1952 Elgin started looking for a lot on which to build. After supper he took me past 1215 Oak Park, the only vacant lot on the block. By the time Elgin came home the next day, he not only liked the lot, but he had bought it. He did a little inquiring and consulted with Mr. Charles Lindsey, an architect, and he felt a house for our family could be put on the lot with nice space for a back lawn. Mr. Lindsey spent many hours helping us in designing our house, and we have never been sorry that we built instead of remodeling and adding on to an already inadequate, small design.

From 1952 until August of 1953 we were preoccupied with house plans and blueprints, which we changed ten thousand times! Charles wanted to please, but he also kept us out of trouble. Elgin worked closely with J.O.

Wilson, the builder, and Charlie. When the house was under roof, Elgin would come home, we would eat, wash dishes, pile in the car, and head for Oak Park. The inside framing was like a slow train through Arkansas. Little by little, we could see that the design was going to be pleasing and spacious. Richard would often ride his tricycle at 1215 Oak Park to watch the workmen work.

I was very particular about the detailing, especially the wood work, baseboards, and finishing around the staircase, fireplace, and hallway. I soon learned that the man that did the detailed work was very meticulous and I did not need to worry.

Many things happened that made me feel that I had indeed come home after many years of living in other states. Francis Hill, a classmate of mine at Maury High School in Dandridge, Tennessee, came to visit me before I had drapes on the windows at Mountain View and Cunningham Street. Francis and Howard were also looking for a house to buy. They bought the only house that we looked at that was structurally sound inside and out, aesthetically pleasing in design, and perfect for a couple, but not for a family of six people. Their house faced Maple Street. We surprised them, as well as ourselves, when we bought the vacant lot behind their house facing Oak Park.

One day I was truly surprised when the door bell rang and I opened the door to find Marshal Vassar from Spring Creek, a small village near Oak Grove, who said, "Ethel, you have been away so long, I almost forgot about you." Marshal did auxiliary work for builders, and he just happened to be in Maryville.

Mother and Daddy came to see us. They were interested in our building a house. Daddy, however, was disappointed that Cam couldn't find one that would meet our needs. I explained that he found houses with room enough for our family, but it would be too expensive and time consuming to make them livable.

Another incident that was indelibly written in my gray matter was the visit by Mrs. D. W. Proffitt in the interest of New Providence Presbyterian Church. That day I had spent every spare moment sewing burlap drapes and had succeeded in finishing one set of pull drapes for the windows facing Mountain View Avenue. The odor from the burlap was less than desirable. I had the windows up and the door open.

I had neglected to plan a menu for the evening meal, but I found some fish in the freezer unit of the refrigerator which I was thawing in hot water. This was creating a fishy odor. The only vegetable in the refrigerator was a small head of cabbage which was steaming slowly on the back burner of the stove. I couldn't describe the odor in my house, or the confusion with the children dashing in and out, or explain the tiny cyanotic infant in a bassinet when I had to excuse myself to care for Johanna. I invited Mrs. Proffitt to come again when I would have drapes on both sets of windows, and hopefully I wouldn't have the conflicting odors gagging us while talking.

I did feel the need to redeem myself from this mixed set of circumstances. When Mrs. Profitt came again, we found we had much in common. She knew the Reverend Gilmore at the Presbyterian Church which we attended while living in Louisville, Kentucky. I told her I had great appreciation for the curriculum material, "Christian Faith and Life." Until I was able to attend church regularly, she would inquire if I had the material for the new quarter. On Mrs. Proffitt's second visit, Johanna had gained back her four pounds of birth weight. I had grown accustomed to her cyanotic circulatory problem which was beginning to clear as she neared her nine-month's gestation.

It was fall and time for the tolling of the school bells. I knew that Beccie would be going to the West Side School where the Municipal Building is today, but I had not met her teacher, Miss Wells. I had, however, stopped by and talked to somebody about our daughter, Beccie Kintner, a third - grader, who would be a nice new face in the schoolroom when school started. The lady discussed with me the overcrowded conditions, but replied, "We will take care of one more student." I appreciated her comment very much. She spoke elegantly about a new school being built for next year. Beccie has always been proud that her fourth grade class was the first to occupy the new Sam Houston School. It was a nice school, and all my children eventually attended Sam Houston Elementary school.

Knowing that kindergarten was not a part of the school system and that Richard was only four-plus years old, I had not anticipated that he would be in school for another two years. However, my neighbor, Mrs. Young, who lived across the street, taught in Mrs. Pesterfield's private pre-school for four-and-five-year-old children. Mrs. Young asked if we would like to enroll Richard. She hastened to add he could ride with her to and from the school. Believe me, this was an unexpected, gracious act that I have always appreciated so much. Richard attended two years. Johanna and Ella attended Mrs. Pesterfield's pre-school one year each.

After years of living away, I had almost forgotten the unbelievable beauty of the multicolored autumn leaves along the Appalachian Plateau. We would take frequent trips to the Great Smoky Mountains National Park to see the steep hills glistening in the sun.

The warning of something to come was evidenced by the cold wind that caused the leaves to fall from the trees to the ground. On one occasion we skipped church and Sunday School to take the children sledding at Clingman's Dome. This was in the late fifties when the hoarfrost blanketed the trees that formed a "winter wonderland" with four feet of snow on the ground. Elgin captured this event with the camera.

In the daily routine of play, accidents would sometimes happen. Johanna, in her attempt to bring in the milk that the milk man left on the porch, stumbled on the doorstep and cut her wrist. She was only twenty months old, and she remembers the blood streaming to the floor. I remember her piteous cry. This was her first accident of any consequence.

Richard and David Carpenter, his favorite playmate, were playing at David's house on Cunningham Street. A crew of men were welding the gutters on the house next door to David's house with the blowtorch on the ground shooting white-hot, invisible flames. When Richard came home, he ran into the blowtorch and his pant leg caught on fire. I heard Richard screaming, and I met him on the porch. The flames had reached the fur trim on his jacket's collar. I put Richard face down on the floor and used the floor mat on the porch to smoother the flames. Richard had a first-degree burn on his neck and a second-degree burn on the inside of his left knee.

One of the most thrilling things that happened to us as a family was the final step in Johanna's adoption. On December 20, 1951, we were to drive to Elkhart, Indiana, to appear before a judge to finalize the adoption consent. That night, an ice storm made roads impassable. We decided to go by train, and around noon we boarded the L. and N. out of Knoxville for an all-night ride. Dad Kintner and Bob met us at Logansport, Indiana, at four A.M. We were cold and hungry, and Mother Kintner had a wonderful breakfast waiting for us. After we tidied ourselves and I prepared Johanna's day's rations, we were off to Elkhart County in Goshen, Indiana, to meet Dick Mehl who would be with us in the last act in finalizing the adoption papers. To say the least it was a meaningful solemn occasion, but so thrilling. Elgin and I were called to the witness stand to answer questions about how we intended to raise Johanna. Bob, Beccie, and Richard watched and listened. Judge Simpson dictated his approval, and the ceremony was over. It was a wonderful feeling to know that we at last had the final papers on all our children.

Dad Kintner's contribution that made part of our trip possible was changing the rear tires on the car to snow tires. The roads were iced over, and the below zero temperature was almost too much exposure for small children. Grandpa wanted to make sure we would navigate and not get waylaid by the roadside.

Bob drove us to Burton's in Elkhart for dinner and once again Yi so graciously fed us and put us up for the night. Bob drove back to North Manchester in the afternoon. The weather conditions were not only cold, but the cold wind made it threatening to be out. Elgin and Richard rode a bus over to Mishawaka, Indiana, and Kenny loaned us his Studebaker to get to South Bend so we could get a train to Chicago. The depot was crowded. I finally found a seat and held Johanna on my lap, but Richard and Beccie sat on the luggage. Elgin was in a long line getting tickets to Chicago. When we arrived, we could sense the difficulty in getting tickets to Knoxville. There were throngs of people in the depot, long lines at the ticket counters, the numbers of people who had been delayed and were just waiting. This proved to be an impossible situation because the train left at eleven-thirty P.M., and Elgin was still in line with no tickets.

Elgin called Delta Airlines, and they had one seat to Knoxville at six-thirty A.M. It was after midnight, and I didn't want to stay in a hotel for the rest of the night and run the risk of added exposure to Johanna in getting to the airport early in the morning by myself. In addition, I felt it best to keep the family together. Elgin called Delta again to see if they had three seats to Cincinnati, from where Johanna and I would go to Knoxville. Yes, they could do this if we came over immediately and claimed the seats for the six A.M. flight. It was cold and eleven P.M. I was three months pregnant. I was carrying seven-month-old Johanna. Beccie had the formula, diaper bag, and a train case. Richard, a three-year-old, had his pillow. Elgin had four suitcases and a bag, standing on the sidewalk waiting for a cab. We were all huddled together trying to protect one another from the bitter cold wind. Our plight was readily evident to a cab driver who pulled up in front of us and told others that he wanted only us to get in. Elgin was sure he didn't tip the cab driver enough. At last we were at the Delta counter, we claimed our tickets for the six A.M. flight, and now the dilemma was whether we should try to put up in the hotel for the rest of the night or stay in the airport. We took the advice of the airline agent and waited all night at the airport.

Richard soon fell asleep. I have forgotten the details I had to go through to get Johanna's bottle warmed, but somebody came to my rescue. She took a bottle of formula and also fell asleep. I made her a bed on a seat out of my coat, and I sat beside her until it was time for us to board for home. Beccie, however, had a wonderful time watching the people go by! She was thrilled she would get to tell her friends about her midnight safari in Chicago. However, she soon announced to her daddy that she wanted a hamburger, french fries, and a coke which she devoured immediately. Around one o'clock she, too, decided to give up and join the rest on the benches. The next morning we were lucky to get checked through on Delta to Knoxville, Tennessee.

I had hoped that we would be in our new house before the baby came, but such was not the case. On July 14, 1952, I went to the hospital around midnight, and Ella was born at 5 A.M. Before I left the delivery room I remembered that she had long black hair. The nurses put a bow on her hair before they brought her out to nurse. In my nursing experience, I had never seen a newborn with that much hair.

When I was discharged from the hospital, Elgin brought all three children, Beccie, Richard, and Johanna, to see their new baby sister, Ella. Elgin preserved this occasion by taking a picture of all four children with Beccie holding Ella.

Needless to say, I was pretty well confined to the house. I tried not to impose on Beccie's play time after school to watch Johanna, but occasionally I did ask her to stroll Johanna in the buggy while I went to the grocery store. I would always take Ella with me. It wasn't long until Beccie's time after school was no longer play time—it was music lessons, scouts, church, and study.

One month later Ella and I flew to Lansing, Michigan, to attend Carol Rundquest's wedding. Elgin drove with the three older children. Beccie was nine years old, Richard four years old, and Johanna one year old. Somehow, somebody closed the car door on Johanna's little finger. When they came to the airport at Lansing, Michigan, to get Ella and me, Elgin was carrying Johanna and she was holding her little finger up so I could see it.

Carol was Elgin's niece, the daughter of his sister Ruth. When we got to Ruth's house I kept Ella upstairs, and I went up often to see about her and feed her. One time I found the middle of the bed empty, and I thought Elgin had gotten her for some reason. When I investigated thoroughly, I found that she had wiggled her way to the back side of the bed and fallen to the floor. Fortunately it was a low bed, and the carpet was soft. I would take Johanna with me when I fed Ella, and she would stroke Ella's black hair and say "Kitty cat, kitty cat." We all came home together in our car.

In August of 1953 we moved in our new house 1215 Oak Park Avenue. This was a wonderful day! I was so happy that Beccie and Richard could have their own bedroom. Of course, we had Johanna in a youth bed and Ella in a crib in the nursery downstairs adjacent to the master bedroom. When I called to Beccie and Richard in the morning I found Richard in with Beccie or Beccie in with Richard. When and why they did this I will never know! In time they became very possessive and proud of their own rooms. They would, however, share with friends and have overnight guests for slumber parties.

Bringing Ella home from the hospital. Beccie is holding Ella, I am holding Johanna, and Richard is wondering why it couldn't have been a boy.

Chapter Ten

Family Living

I would be misleading you if I gave the impression that I had been a model parent or that I was right in all my decisions and practices in raising my family. I hereby acknowledge my inadequacies as wife, mother, parent, grandmother, and/or educator.

Nevertheless, I realized that nurture and nature can be enriched just as school curriculum and teaching techniques can inspire young students to be better students. The old saying, "There are two sides to every coin," is especially true for the nature of children and the nurturing of children.

Human nature is a quality with which one seems to be born, whereas, nurturing is giving love and guidance during growth, development, and maturation.

For several years, my anticipation of family living became my reason for being, and it seemed only natural that I labored in the field of nurturing my children on their pilgrimage to adulthood. I grew up with the idea that child-rearing came naturally. But I soon learned what is taught is not always what is learned, and what is learned is not always what is desired. I admitted to myself that I had four children with different natures, needing different types of nurturing. The challenge was awesome, but I was young and a little naive, therefore willing to struggle with the daily happenings. However early on, I did not yet have the concept that God had asked me, above all else was a parent, to be faithful to the task of family living. My faith journey at that time was in its infancy. But as I labored in my "vineyard" I learned more about how to care for my very own.

Moreover, Elgin and I were on a roller coaster ride with a few surprises along the way, but we were never significantly derailed. Just going along for the ride seemed like fun, because the experience of family living belongs to all ages. The Biblical story of the first family in Genesis gives evidence of starts and stops, ups and downs, love and sorrow, understanding and confusion. But, finally, Abraham and Sarah were faithful to their calling.

Sharing activities and celebrations while wandering in the wilderness was a wonderful way to learn about one another and how to manage the stresses and strains of parenthood.

Elgin and I came to know that simple celebration and repeated activities were important for the nurturing and nature of our children: birthday parties, anniversaries, holiday festivities—Thanksgiving, Christmas, and Easter—Girl Scouts, Boy Scouts, church choir, music lessons, camping, hiking, swimming parties, vacations, slumber parties, and the evening meal in the dining room helped to establish a pattern of decorum for life.

We moved in our new house, 1215 Oak Park Avenue, in August of 1953. Beccie was ten years old, Richard was five, Johanna was two, and Ella was one. My days were centered around nurturing, housework, cooking, laundry, sewing, and car pooling. However, for the most part my participation in car pooling was only in the afternoons. Elgin left the house at 7:30 in the morning, and he stopped at the top of Mountain View and Cunningham Street. Beccie went to high school. The next year Richard went to Sam Houston. Most of the time Richard wanted to ride his bike. When Johanna and Ella went to Mrs. Pesterfield's they also rode with Elgin to Mrs. Young's house. In the afternoon I was responsible for picking up those that needed a ride home. Car pooling wasn't a problem for me as much as rides to extra curricular activities.

Before I enrolled Johanna and Ella in Kindergarten, I was pregnant. Unfortunately, I had a spontaneous abortion at about three months. Dr. Lambeth told me I had an inadequate implantation. When Johanna and Ella were three and four respectively, I was pregnant again.

Elgin and I slowly came to the conclusion that it was impossible to get everything done, and we got a live-in assistant to help with the housekeeping and the children. Sarah Caughron was sixteen and a high school dropout, but she wanted domestic work. At first, I felt like I had taken on another child, but after I acquainted her with the routine, she proved me wrong. It was such a relief when I had to pick up Beccie or Richard or both for music lessons, church choir, or a scout meeting that I could safely leave Johanna and Ella with Sarah. Another assignment that became a constant for Sarah was that she would take Johanna, Ella, and Richard to the basement for play while I cooked the evening meal. After dinner Sarah would load the dishwater, but it took her a long time to fine tune a kitchen cleanup.

In preparation for "nighty-by," Sarah would bath Johanna and Ella, and then I would take over for a story or a little rocking chair treatment. Sarah would watch "The Lone Ranger" with Richard and then it would be time for his bath, homework, and to bed. Beccie was self-sufficient, and I could depend on her taking care of her homework and her after school activities.

In spring of 1954, we had so much for which to be thankful. Everybody according to age, size, and accomplishment had weathered the storm in work, play, and excitement during the fall and winter of 1953. Spring brought green grass on the front and back lawns, shrubs and trees were budding. Sarah had made herself indispensable. Elgin's work in the laboratory at the Blount Memorial Hospital was progressing. The children had many friends in the community, church, and school, and the house had surpassed our expectations for comfortable family living. We installed an above-ground swimming pool for the children that was eighteen feet in diameter and three-and-a-half feet high. My stomach was growing and I was crowding D-day.

The swimming pool served as a wonder recreation not only for my children but also for their friends. I reserved the right to schedule special times for special occasions, but it turned out that no occasion was special without their friends. The pool had a slide which they kept greased with wax paper for extra thrills. Unfortunately, Beccie had almost outgrown the pool when it was new. However, between dusk and dark Beccie and her friends had private parties as often as they wanted around the pool and/or in the pool. Richard was willing to swim with Johanna, Ella, and their friends during the day as much as he wanted. The girls loved having him because he taught them how to swim—Ella in particular. This helped me a lot since Richard would watch after the little ones. Nevertheless, I served as life guard every single day when the pool was operating. As Richard grew older, I reserved the late afternoon and evening for Richard and his friends. Ella and Beccie had birthdays in summer and were the only two for whom I could legitimately have a swimming party, but I had a special swimming party for each of the children sometime during the summer. The pool would accommodate about eight to ten children from five-to-ten years of age. Later on, Richard was on the swimming team at Green Meadow Country Club, and little by little the girls outgrew the pool. We have many pictures that speak loud and clear about the swimming pool parties. Each of the children as their own stories to tell.

In early April, Elgin and I went downtown to get a few items for the new baby for whom the time was drawing near. In getting out of the car, I slipped on a well-used cud of tobacco and fractured my coccyx. I began to have contractions, and I was hospitalized for a few days. On May fifth I went into labor, and at three A.M. I had *abruptio placenta* where the placenta separates from the uterus before delivery. Evelyn Jean did not expand her lungs, and had to be resuscitated. She died at midnight May ninth. I got out of bed, dressed, and came home with Elgin. Sarah had gotten along pretty well with the children and the housekeeping. We waited until morning to tell the family about Evelyn Jean's death. It was hard for Beccie and Richard to go to school that day, but they did. The next afternoon we had a graveside service for her at the French Broad Church of the Brethren. Beccie and Richard went, but I stayed home with Johanna and Ella.

Beccie and Richard looked forward to having a new baby as much as Elgin and I did. Johanna and Ella were too little to realize much about what was going on. However, we had Evelyn Jean brought to the house from McCammon-Ammons Funeral home. Johanna remembered seeing her and thought we had the funeral at the house. It took me a while to get over the loss of what was to be our last baby. In time, I got each of the girls a baby-sized doll on which to use the clothes that had been given to us and the out-grown baby dresses that once belonged to Johanna and Ella.

Sarah stayed with us until school started. Johanna and Ella were five and four respectively. I missed Sarah a lot, but I was ready to take over the house and care for the children. The girls had friends on the street with whom they played, either at our house or at the house of the Badgett twins. The twins and Ella were the same age, and little Nan Badgett was thrown in for good measure.

Beccie was a Girl Scout and Zelma Smith and I were leaders of the intermediate troop for three years. We met in the basement at our house. Campouts in the Great Smoky Mountains were a common occurrence in the spring and fall. Hiking was a favorite pastime for the weekends. Richard wanted to be a Cub Scout, but it seemed that no mother in his group of friends wanted to be a Cub Scout leader. I was determined that he would have the opportunity, and I volunteered to be the leader. Beccie's troop became Senior Scouts as did many other Girl Scout troops in Blount county, and many girls wanted to do senior scouting. Again, leadership became a problem, and Elgin agreed to be the leader of Blount County's Senior Girl Scout Troop. They continued to meet at our house in the evenings. Richard's Cub Pack met in the basement and back yard of our house on Mondays after school. We started out with ten boys, but by the second year we had lost two. The mothers were nice about furnishing refreshments, and some of the fathers took the boys on outings—fishing, rafting, hiking, and on campouts. After three years, eight fine, well-qualified boys joined the Boy scout program at new Providence Presbyterian Church. Richard excelled and won the Regional Award offered for decorum in uniform, polite behavior, and badges earned. Eventually he became an Eagle Scout, and earned the God and My Country Award.

Beccie, Susan Callaway, and Barbara Shields from Elgin's Senior Girl Scout Troop qualified for the International Senior Roundup in Colorado Springs April 1959. The Roundup is designed to give Senior Girls a sense of belonging to a strong and unified organization. Nine thousand girls and/or leaders from around the world were in attendance.

Elgin kept a health record on the family and in 1957 he recorded the following:

Ella is in Kindergarten five years old, weighs thirty-six pounds, and is forty-two inches tall, Johanna is six years old weighs forty pounds and is forty-four inches tall. Johanna started to big school and complained the first day that she couldn't read her book. Richard is nine years old, weighs sixty-four pounds, fifty-five inches tall, and in fourth grade. Beccie is fourteen years old, weighs ninety-three pounds, sixty-three inches tall, and in eighth grade. Ethel is forty-three years old, weighs 110 pounds. Elgin is forty years old and weighs 157 pounds. Ethel skinned her knee. Beccie and Elgin were dealing with psoriasis, Ella had impetigo. Beccie had a sore throat and enlarged spleen—out of school for several days. Johanna had croup, and lost her first tooth. Ethel fainted on arising. Richard had chills and fever; he was given penicillin. Elgin had hay fever from maple trees. Beccie had polyarthritis from camping out; she was given cortisone. Johanna had pneumonia and Ella and Johanna had measles. Ella learned to do dead man's float, and Johanna jumped from 3rd diving board at Green Meadow Country Club and swam out. Johanna had sore throat and Ella saw Dr. Carpenter for an evaluation of her feet for high arches. Richard had fever and pain. Elgin and Ella had flu. Mother Pritchett had heart block and was hospitalized. Ethel had D & C. Beccie had swollen finger joints. Johanna fell from top of bunk bed hurting her forearm and broke her nose; she was given an anesthetic to set her nose, Ella has a runny nose and we all got flu shots. Beccie had a cold, Ella had fever of 105, Richard has fever, also. All had temperatures of 101 or above today, and the best guess is influenza. Ella is on colace, and Johanna is in trouble with Latin. Ella is vomiting, complaining of earache, and was treated with penicillin and sulfa.

This scenario was on-going process until the children were grown.

Elgin ran the laboratory by himself from 1951 until 1957. The Alcoa, Blount County, and Maryville communities were growing, and the Blount County Medical Society was expanding. When Elgin would attend the state, national, and international medical meetings—which were very important in keeping up with the latest in laboratory medicine—he would take the microscope and have the slides flown in. He started his day by reading and dictating the information to his secretary at Blount Memorial Hospital. Elgin wasn't quite ready for a full-time partner, but he couldn't offer the service that was necessary for the doctors and the hospitals because of the increase in volume of work to be done.

In December of 1957, Dr. Edward Kelman arrived as Elgin's first partner. They rotated the services,, established a forty-hour work week, took turns on call, and decided that each would take a month vacation. This was the first time that Elgin had ever had any time off-duty. This was a wonderful feeling for the family.

It was sheer luxury to think that we could leave on vacation and be gone a month. We decided to take a trip to the west coast. The trip was justified because we would attend a family get-together and a family wedding.

This was during the time the National Parks and National Forests were being up-dated and equipped for tourist attractions and camping. Self-guided tours, evening programs, recreational equipment, and museums were being established for the convenience of the hale and hardy outdoorsman wanting to see the country and enjoy the parks. This happened to be the Kintner's family forté.

Getting equipment together for a family of six to travel three thousand miles to go camping, with Ella at four years old, Johanna at five, Richard at nine and Beccie at thirteen was a little frightening to say the least.

Elgin and I decided to buy a Helite utility trailer, the top of which was the size of a traditional mattress and on which Elgin and I slept. At that time the Helite was the champion of trailers on the road. The waterproof tent folded out into a fifty-square-foot space with an aluminum lid that let down inside the tent which housed five wooden boxes for storage and clothing. The outside space—like the inside space—housed the cooking and eating equipment, ice chest, stove, and plastic dish pans and wash basins. We had room for a trunk sixteen inches in height in which to house our good clothes. Richard had a pop-up tent with a front door the same size as the door to the trailer, which expanded the floor space in which children could sleep. Johanna and Ella took turns sleeping in Richard's tent. We had warm clothing for night sleeping, including scarves, gloves, wool socks, and fleece-lined sleepers, sleeping bags, and wool blankets. I secretively told myself that if we tried camping and it didn't work, we could sell the trailer, hop an airplane, and go home.

Dr. Kelman came to take over the lab while we were gone. We were packed and left Maryville at eight o'clock on a Saturday morning in 1957. We stopped in Nashville to say hello to my sister, Erlene Hanson. As Elgin drove out of her drive, the back end of the trailer struck the gate post—our first accident, and a good lesson early on. I believe we crossed the Mississippi River and camped in Arkansas the first night. We followed the mid-western route through Oklahoma, Kansas, Nebraska, and Wyoming. We spent some time in Yellowstone National Park and the Grand Tetons. Every day was so exciting and every part was more so, and we all became addicted to camping. We had a roaring campfire every night. Our first trip was so successful that we did a camping trip every year.

In July of 1958 we took another west coast trip. We followed the southern route to Disneyland. We followed the coast line to San Francisco, California; Portland, Oregon; and Olympia, Wenatchee, and Port Angeles, Washington. We were gone one month and sights and sounds we observed were breathtaking. Olympia National Park was beautiful to behold. The rain forest was laden with Sitka spruce which produces long, spiny, green cones. It was a big thrill to visit Elgin's brothers and their families who lived in the Pacific northwest. We headquartered at Quentin's in Port Angeles. Quentin and Chris had a summer home on a lake with water sports for the combined families with four children each. This was more than fun! In the evenings we would have a roaring fire in the fireplace. For the evening meal Quentin would broil a thirty-pound salmon over an open fire using his own "witch's brew." No one ever knew what was in it, but somehow, I didn't care. I savored the odor and the taste. Quentin did this more than once for us, and we shall never forget. Our camping trips have helped the cousins to know one another and keep in touch.

Doing a camping trip every summer was something the children look forward. Camping became very popular and the parks, national or state, were struggling to keep up with the demand of the tourists. We were always thrilled when we didn't have to go to the overflow camp ground. Camping equipment and camping trailers became more adapted to the use for which they were to serve. In our own case we used two-inch Naugahyde pads under the sleeping bags. It is essential for a month's camping trip that everybody be comfortable and warm at night!

When we felt we had enough experience in camping, we updated our camping equipment and on June 7, 1963, we took off for Alaska. Beccie was in nurse's training at the University of Tennessee and couldn't leave before vacation time, but she flew out to Washington State to meet us.

We shall never forget the mighty rushing waters as we drove through Canada. When we came to Calgary we were beginning to get the picture of rugged landscape, steep mountain peaks, fewer services along the highway, and this continued until we boarded the first ocean ship at Prince Rupert to navigate the deep waters offering an alternate service for pedestrians, airline passengers, and cars. Incidentally, when we got to Calgary, we were half way to Alaska. A sobering bit of information. I was truly shocked when I learned that the hull of the ship accommodated 250 assorted types of conveyances. We were able to get into the main part of our trailer and in the wee hours the children gave up and decided to take a nap.

We had choice seats near the front of the ship and the scenery was like nothing we had ever seen before. The whales were churning the sky blue water and exposing their fin-like tails that vibrated the ship. The moon was visible, but it was daylight until well after midnight. The snow on the mountain peaks glistened, and the visibility at night time was striking, grand, and unusual. We were advised that we would be stopping at Ketchikan for loading and unloading. More vehicles were added to the bow. A Boy Scout master boarded with twenty boys who livened things up to the tune of noisy. The next stop was Wrangell, where we lost our Boy Scouts, and after that was Sitka, where the ship was to be in dock for two hours while the passengers visited the historical sights. It was eleven o'clock and we were to be back at the dock at two A.M.

It was a short mile from the dock into town. However, X marked the spot on the map of the things we wanted to see. It was another half-mile to the National Historical Park. The most interesting thing for the children, especially Richard, were the totem poles. There were hundreds. Richard remembered the Indian lore well enough to know that a particular symbol represented a particular Indian tribe. We stopped at the white, wooden, Russian Orthodox Church. It was a modest white wooden structure in the center of town. At the back of the church was a large stone mounted on a rock with the following inscription: *The Russian stone was used by citizens of Sitka to sharpen tools from 1830 until 1926. It was turned by water power from the Swan Lake.*

As we rushed back to town we ran into a woman, and when she found out we were from Maryville, Tennessee, she immediately asked about Maryville College from which she was a graduate. She married a minister, and they were connected with the Sheldon Jackson Presbyterian College in Sitka, Alaska. She invited us to their house to share in a farewell party for a group of young people engaged in a work program for the college. We thanked her very much, but told her that we had to be back at the dock at 2 o'clock. She insisted that we eat with her family and said that they would drive us back. In passing, we remarked that we were sorry that the museum was closed, "Oh," she exclaimed, "I have the key," and we were able to visit the Sheldon Jackson Museum's fantastic showing of artifacts of bygone days used by early natives of the region.

This was an unusually hospitable act, and we enjoyed it thoroughly. A mere "thank you" seemed sterile and inadequate. They were excited over our efforts to do the Alaskan-Alcan Highway. When we disembarked at Skagway, we were given a package of food to take with us.

We soon learned that the tires we had on the trailer were no match for the rough gravel stone and rugged ruts that we were to crisscross before reaching the blacktop that extended a few miles east of Fairbanks. Even then the blacktop was rutted from the thaws and freezes—an impossible problem on the Alcan Highway! We had two flat tires on the blacktop before we got to the Fairbanks camp ground. We had the sum total of fifteen flat tires on the trip. It was a big thrill when we drove downtown in the center of Fairbank's town square to read the sign post that listed the mileage and said, when interpreted, *You are closer to Tokyo than New York City.*

Fortunately, Richard was old enough to help Elgin change a tire. One thing that surprised us was the repair shops scattered along the highway, and one could always get help. In the '60s few people with trailers had traveled on Alcan Highway, but increased traffic otherwise was not unusual.

Disregarding the flat tires, we had so much to see and enjoy that we almost forgot that a flat tire was an inconvenience. The nights were cold, but we were prepared for cold weather. One night, however, the thermometer was to drop into the teens. Elgin was preparing the bedrolls for the girls and decided that Johanna needed a warmer one, so it might be a good idea to get two more wool blankets. Beccie had always been sensitive to cold weather, and Elgin wanted to be sure everybody was sleeping warm.

The University of Fairbanks was experimenting with dairy cattle to see if the tundra would be sufficient for grazing during the short summer months, and if harvested would the tundra—supplemented with grain—bring milk production sufficient to make dairy farming profitable. Dairy products were very expensive, and were not available to tourists at all. The other experiment under way was plots of ground for garden vegetables. There were no fresh vegetables on the market.

We bought canned milk, which was curdled but sweet. The children closed their eyes to be able to use it on breakfast cereal. We have pictures of the experimental land that the horticulturists had under cultivation. Unfortunately, the cold winters and short growing season probably defeated both projects. I never heard, but have often wondered! However before we left home, we were advised about the high prices, the scarcity of food, and the rugged Alcan Highway in Alaska.

While in Calgary, Alberta, Canada, we bought a good supply of canned food and non-perishable food before leaving for Alaska. We could buy frozen loaves of bread, bacon, and sausage in Alaska. I stocked the pantry with non-perishables at Fairbanks before we left for the most anticipated part of our Alaskan trip.

All along the way we enjoyed views and vistas that perhaps we will never see again. We saw caribou, buffalo, wild horses, bighorn sheep, and herds of elk grazing on tundra. But by far the most exotic view and overnight stay was our campout at the foot of Mt. McKinley National Park. We left Fairbanks on a narrow dirt road that was rutty and curvy, rugged and steeped, with the massive Talkeetina Mountains on the right side; and on the left side, a narrow meadow allowed room every few miles for observation platforms to view the 20,320 feet high mass of glitter if the atmosphere was clear and if the sun happened to shine. That day the good Lord was with us. We stopped twice to try to comprehend what we were seeing and to take pictures. The clear sky and the sunshine seemed to magnify the luster to an unbelievable brilliance.

Few people were in the camp site. We could choose where we wanted to pitch our tent for the night. Wander Lake was clear, still, and in landscape with the weather—mild, no wind, and the sunset streaked the sky with rainbow colors, but it was still daylight at two o'clock in the morning. The bluejays dive bombed us, and the mosquitos swarmed all over us. But fortunately, the mosquitos were too large and clumsy to bite. The bluejays kept up a squawking sound until we went to bed. We stayed up until dark set in at three o'clock in the morning. We got up around nine o'clock, had breakfast, packed up, and retraced the terrain back to Fairbanks.

The next morning we headed back, counting the mile posts in reverse. It was tedious driving, but we were awe-stricken by the scenery and wildlife along the way. The children had lots of curiosity about the camping facilities at the next stop for the night. After several days we crossed over into Canada's Yukon Territory, went though British Columbia, and spent one night at Lake Louise. The hotel is framed by the lake in the front and the Rocky Mountains in the back. We had been there before, but this time the campground was outfitted with cooking stoves. I did a pot roast with vegetables, and the children roasted marshmallows over the campfire. We went to the evening lectures. The next day we crossed over into Alberta and spent the night in a campground near Calgary. I did an inventory of the spartan pantry and bought food and ice for the chest. We were getting in territory where we could make up for the lack of fresh fruits, vegetables, and dairy products. We crossed over at North Dakota into the United States. We visited parks and did a lot of sight seeing in South Dakota, Nebraska, Kansas, Missouri, and finally Tennessee. We were willing to drive eight hundred miles the last day to get home.

The children were growing and advancing in school with activities and interests in addition to book learning. All were scout enthusiasts. Richard sang in youth church choir, competed in swimming and won several times, served as life guard at Fontana Lake, and served as counselor at Camp Pellissippi. Beccie played the violin, took piano and organ lessons, and was an avid Girl Scout. Johanna went to Sewanee Summer Music Center for two summers. She was first chair clarinet in middle school, junior high school, and high school. Johanna and Ella completed the intermediate level of Girl Scouts. Ella played the oboe, went to Sewanee Summer Music Camp one summer, sang in church choir, and took piano lessons. Both Johanna and Ella played in Maryville High Band.

By far the most enjoyable family living for the Tennessee Kintners was the year from 1963 to 1964, when Ernst Leitner from Nickelsdorf, Austria, came to stay as an exchange student through the International Christian Youth Program. He was to be a senior at Maryville High school. Ernst was sponsored by the Westminster Fellowship of New Providence Presbyterian Church, a youth group of about forty teenagers. In the rolling of the dice, the Kintners were selected to be the host family. We were delighted, and Richard was especially overjoyed. Ernst arrived a month before school started, and we wanted him to see as much of the United States as possible, so we took a two-week camping trip to New England with a two-day stopover at the Worlds Fair at New York where Ernst saw the Austrian exhibit. We went as far as the Canadian border, and stopped in Washington D.C. on our way home. We got home a few days before school started.

Ernst had a lot of adjustments to make. Elgin and I marveled at his behavioral patterns—he was always mannerly and did the right thing. He was never in the way, but always there when we needed him. Ernst was forced to live in the Kintner family with one boy and three girls when he had one brother back home. At the time Ernst was here, Beccie was twenty-one in nurse's training at University of Tennessee. Richard was seventeen, Johanna was fourteen, and Ella was thirteen. Ernst turned seventeen while he was here. We pre-arranged a phone call while we were at church and soon after we got home the phone rang. Elgin answered and said, "Ernst, it is for you." It was his mother on the line, and Ernst forgot and began talking in English. Elgin could tell something was wrong and said, "Ernst, talk in German." We all had a good laugh over that one.

We wanted to do one more sightseeing trip with Ernst before he left the United States. Unfortunately, Beccie was at the University, Richard was a counselor at Camp Pellissippi, and Johanna was at music camp. Ella, Ernst, Elgin, and I set out for California shortly after school was out. We were gone a month, covering twenty states. We stopped in Houston, Texas and saw the Phillies defeat the Astros in the new stadium. We spent two days hiking in the Grand Canyon, and I shall never forget how steep it was coming back. In the evening we would hear lectures by the park naturalist. This trip included Yosemite, Yellowstone, the Grand Tetons, and the Black Hills national Monument. While there we saw two outdoor dramas; one a passion play depicting the last five days in the life of Christ, and the other a production of the last days of the Sioux Chief Crazy Horse. On Saturday evening in Cody, Wyoming, we took in a wild west rodeo show. Sunday morning we got dressed up in our Sunday best and drove down the main street, parked in a church parking lot, and went in. The congregation was celebrating the seventy-fifth anniversary of Wyoming's statehood and was all decked out in frontier finery. We felt a little foolish. We didn't have to tell them we were tourists passing through.

One of the sights that Ernst appreciated most was the Mount Rushmore National Memorial with the four Presidents carved in stone—George Washington, Abraham Lincoln, Theodore Roosevelt, and Woodrow Wilson.

Elgin and I visited Ernst and his wife Inge in 1972. We had Sunday dinner with Ernst's folks in Nickelsdorf, Austria. Ernst and Inge put us in their car and drove us around the countryside for a week in Austria and Switzerland. We spent the nights in tourist homes. Ernst knew how to find the unique places—like the one where we were served breakfast on the upstairs balcony.

We had our last dinner together in Zurich, and the next morning Elgin and I rode a train to Munich. This trip was business combined with pleasure. Elgin gave a paper on "Acid/Base Balance" to the World Congress of Clinical and Anatomic Pathology. He did his work in his own laboratory, and it was published in textbooks for medical students and researchers. Another attraction was the Olympics, which had to end with a bombing by terrorists. Before we came home we flew to Paris, London, and Dublin, Ireland. We rented a car and drove to Belfast in northern Ireland. This was during a period of IRA violence, and we were very uncomfortable, to say the least. Sand bags, armored vehicles, and armed guards with machine guns were keeping people out and keeping order. It was a good feeling when we drove through the gate safely on our way back to Donegal. However, the headlines in the paper the next morning told about a bombing at the gate that we came through. We ended our trip, turned in the car, and hopped on the airplane, and came home.

In the fall of 1996, Ernst, his wife Inge, and their daughter Kerstin came to Richard's high school class reunion of 1964. Ernst wanted Inge and Kerstin to visit the house where we lived when Ernst lived with us. It wasn't enough to see the first floor and the upstairs, Inge and Kerstin wanted to open the door and see the bedroom where Ernst slept. The basement was a downstairs den with two bedrooms and connecting bath. The boys, Richard and Ernst, lived downstairs, the girls lived upstairs, and the old folks lived on the first floor. Elgin and I have fond memories of those days. We have lots of pictures, letters, stories, and personal memories deeply imbedded in our hearts and minds. Today, Ernst Leitner is the manager of Austrian Airlines for five European countries.

Elgin and I.

Richard, Ella, Beccie, and Johanna on a camping trip.

Beccie, Richard, Johanna, and Ella on a hike.

Chapter Eleven

Where To From Here?

My Appalachian journey seems to be characterized by a sense of awe, because I am a wife, a mother, and a grandmother. As I moved from one stage in my life to another, I realized that Americans are in transition, and the people of Appalachia are encountering uncertainties and often difficulties that seem insurmountable. As I look back, my greatest opportunities for self-renewal and new growth occurred in the changes brought about by technology.

If I had anything in my favor, it was that there were few stresses and stains of parenthood that I experienced and many joys and pleasures. I was furnished with the necessities of life and many things that bordered on luxuries that helped to modify stressful situations. Elgin and I shared the struggles involved in family living.

To answer the question—where to from here?—let me now reflect on the days when the children were approaching adulthood. Johanna and Ella were in high school as a junior and as a senior, respectively, Richard was in college, and Beccie was married. With two out on their own, it seemed that I had no spare time which to call my own. I felt the need for a change in whatever it was that seemed so important. I was still working to get everything done before I lay me down to sleep. I realized I needed to do something to make my days a little less stressful, a little more meaningful, and not quite so monotonous. One day, I remembered what my mother said when she, my two sisters, and I were working feverishly to complete a project. I just can't recall what the project was, but mother stopped and said, "Girls, we are going to quit; if there is no tomorrow we don't need it."

This helped me to evaluate my household and my own activities and make some choices that would be enjoyable to me and, perhaps, beneficial to others.

I became involved in church work through the New Providence Presbyterian Church—the women's work in particular. What I enjoyed most was tutoring underprivileged children in neighborhood schools and the Home Avenue and Sunny Brook chapels, which were sponsored by the Presbyterian Church. This was very rewarding. I would choose two or three students and meet with them twice a week. I was contacted by a teacher who told me my students were taking more interest in their school work. This pleased me very much.

I was a member of Blount County Medical Auxiliary. This organization did a lot of community volunteer work in schools, at children's home, with the Red Cross and community health programs, and had a Doctor's Day celebration in honor of our husbands once a year. The auxiliary committee worked on legislative matters which were in harmony with the American Medical Association. We gave scholarships to boys and girls interested in medicine or nursing.

One of our objectives was to promote mutual understanding and culti-vate friendly relations among physicians' families. All the doctors' wives were personally involved in this endeavor. The Medical Auxiliary had din-ners and bridge parties once every month in alternate homes. Doctors' fam-ilies were recognized for special occasions, such as the birth of a new baby, a new doctor coming to town, when a doctor retired, and for special achievements.

This was back in the '50s when the Blount County Medical Association numbered in the thirties. The Medical Auxiliary met once a month. We had special programs in relation to the purpose and objectives for which the Medical Auxiliary existed, that of advancing medicine and health education on the local, state, and national level.

In the early '60s I enrolled in the University of Tennessee for a refresh-er course in nursing. Over time that led to a bachelor of science degree in public health, with a secondary teacher's certificate. By this time the chil-dren were launched. Elgin and I were proud of their accomplishments, but somehow our role in family life had changed from nurturing to a stabiliz-ing force. We had been responsible, as all parents are, for our children's moral and religious education. But we also realized that an understanding of a meaningful life is not suddenly acquired at a particular age.

Personally, I believe parenting behavior is learned by osmosis and through precept and example. Elgin and I felt that our parents passed on to us the Christian virtues and the moral imperatives for which we passed the torch. We both admit that parents are limited in what they can do at times to change behavior. But acknowledging the church and community as our extended family, God's grace as freely given, and the Holy Spirit as our comforter, Elgin and I managed to hold fast, and today we have a loving, caring, compassionate family of which we are proud.

Volunteer work in the educational field seemed to have magnetized me. I served as a volunteer tutor for the Job Corps, post-World War II, for three years at a federally administered National Employment Training and Teaching Center in Townsend, Tennessee, for disadvantaged youth sixteen to twenty-five years old. Two-thirds of 250 boys couldn't read or write well enough to write home or to read a letter from home. The boys were required to write a letter home every week and read a letter from home if they got one. The Job Corps appealed to the churches for volunteer help. Volunteers were assigned three boys each and, we could come once a week or more often if we wanted too.

I became intrigued with the program. The slogan was "Work, Play, and Educate." All the boys worked in Great Smoky Mountain National Park until high noon. The afternoon was spent in education and recreation. The educational program was a self-directed program with materials from grades one through twelve. It was possible for the boys to get a Graduate Equivalency Diploma (GED) under the self-directed, self-paced, diagnostic, prescriptive type of teaching and learning. The boys were evaluated for basic educational needs and familiarized with the library that housed books appropriate for their reading levels. There were special books that spoke to adult problems and special interests—not Dick and Jane, Baby Ray, or the basic readers like they had when they started to school. This was an all new teaching and learning technique, and some of the boys were frustrated with the design. However, students reported periodically to the head master or the one part-time school teacher that came from three o'clock until six o'clock three days a week to give help and make suggestions. Volunteers came in the afternoons on whatever day suited them best.

My three boys were at different levels in reading, math, and English and wanted as much help as they could get. However, I always attended to the letter writing and letter reading first as was my assignment. One of my boys never got a letter from home. This depressed me, and I could only guess that his parents were illiterate. He was seventeen years old, had dropped out of school in fifth grade, and was reading on second-grade level. During the last year the Job Corps was at Townsend, I went an extra afternoon to help my boys on reading, English, and math. One of my students was moving toward the GED, and I wanted him to achieve that goal. Two boys achieved the GED the first year the camp was established. This served as an incentive for all the boys. All three of my students were moving slowly on the graph in reading and writing, but it was hard for them to become accustomed to the self-directed learning system. The adults' self-concept of self-directed learning for the Job Corps is in direct conflict with the traditional practice of teachers making assignments, grading papers, lecturing, giving grades, and being responsible for the students' progress.

The learning situation created for the boys was self-evident. They knew on what level they were reading, they knew their own writing skills, they also knew that reading and writing supports all other learning. They knew that to improve English skills and math skills they needed to practice English and math skills. Moreover, since they had not learned how to work on a particular skill in English and in math, they could work sets of problems and punctuate sentences that represented the skills needed and check the answers, which were always available to them. They had textbooks with detailed examples and procedures on all levels of learning and in all subject areas.

The Job Corps boys were given the tools for learning, they were provided with the information about their own level of mastery and the time to study, and a conducive climate in which to learn.

In the fall of 1969, the Alcoa, Blount County, and Maryville Schools created a Nation Youth Corps (NYC) for school dissidents to satisfy the legislation that the youth in Blount County would be returned to Blount County from what ever institution they might have been assigned. The students would go to school in the mornings and work in the community at minimum wage for three hours in the afternoon.

I was asked by the Alcoa, Blount County, and Maryville Schools system to take a class of twenty-three students, sixteen years old to twenty-seven years old, for basic skill improvement from eight o'clock in the morning until twelve o'clock noon. I was a little hesitant, but after talking to the director of vocational education, I decided to give it a try.

In the parlance of the laity, the program was known as partnership learning between the business world and the Alcoa Blount County, and Maryville Schools. All students were school dropouts. All were experiencing grave difficulty in society's expectations which takes for granted that all students will achieve reading, writing, and computational skills in the lower grades. All the NYC students lived in Blount County, and in the past had been connected with Alcoa, Blount County, or Maryville Schools.

Having learned about the alternate teaching program from the federal administered National Employment Training and Teaching Center in Townsend, Tennessee, I wanted to find out more about the teaching and learning changes being made in the school systems.

I went to the learning lab at the University of Tennessee to see if I could combine the format of the federal Job Corps to the traditional school materials that I was supposed to use. I learned that the learning lab concept was developed for the federal Job Corps, and the school systems were to use the self-directed learning techniques for Adult Basic Education. The director of the learning lab at the University told me he would be glad to evaluate my students for levels of proficiency in English, math, and reading. He would also teach me how to interpret the results so I could place my students in materials that would be both achievable and challenging. What more could I ask!

I explained to my students the advantages of self-directed learning and said that with their permission we would forget about "schoolish" ways of learning and substitute an individualized learning process.

My students were grateful that they would not be doing traditional classroom work where grades were more important than learning. They were pleased not to be competing against one another, and they were glad to be responsible for their own improvements on their own level working at their own speed. They were delighted they would be of service to one another without being accused of cheating. They were shocked that the old authority-obedience relationship between student and teacher was never used in their classroom. My students were obedient, and the officer assigned to me came by to see why I hadn't needed him. I told him to ask my students. I left the room while he talked to the students.

Unfortunately, the Job Corp's program didn't get under way until October, and the designated money ran out in April. My students responded to the new learning techniques in surprising ways. Some were glad they could be free, but were a little embarrassed because of their low-level basic skills. Most of my students needed to be rescued from the frustration of pause, word omitted, word fabrication, word-by-word delay, facial grimacing, and the mental fatigue when reading. Some wanted to work toward a GED because they had been denied training programs because they did not have a high school diploma.

For my own curiosity and satisfaction, I turned my basement into a school room for the rest of the school year and during the summer. Monday, Wednesday, and Thursday evenings after the dinner hour, students were welcome to come for help. About four students came at least once a week, but Sue came on a regular schedule. She was adamant about achieving the GED. At times as a facilitator in self-directed learning, I felt frustrated that my students went to the University of Tennessee to take eight exams that were graded by computer. At that stage, I was still learning about the program myself. I did not have all the materials written specifically for self-directed programs, and it was very time-consuming to improvise. However, Sue passed the GED two weeks before school started and passed with an average of eighty-five. She was overjoyed to be the first student to achieve a GED in Blount County.

In self-directed learning, the teacher no longer sees his or her role as being primarily that of a transmitter of knowledge. Conversely, in self-directed learning the teacher becomes a facilitator in which he or she assists the students in assessing strengths and weaknesses in basic skills to build a foundation for future learning. It is really frustrating for a tenth grade student to be given a tenth grade reading assignment when he is reading on a forth-grade level. This did not happen in my classroom. All of my students were at different levels in three subject areas: English, math, and reading. Assignments were made according to the level of achievement in all three subject areas.

In fall of 1970, the Alcoa, Blount County, and Maryville Schools combined the Job Corps with an Adult Basic Educational (ABE) program. I was asked to set up a learning program appropriate for adults over sixteen years of age up to whatever age an adult wanted to return to the halls of learning. This called for more education on my part, and I hit the halls of learning at the masters level at the University of Tennessee.

I set up the learning lab type of instruction for Alcoa, Blount County, and Maryville Schools and served as teacher/coordinator for twelve years. I used the self-paced, self-directed type of teaching and learning. Students were monitored for progress or the lack of progress. We considered the lack of progress a serious problem, and we talked to the students to get information. My philosophy was that a high percentage of all students can learn skills sufficient for entry-level jobs for the twenty-first century.

We used a graph as a grading tool, and students were praised for simple improvements. If they aspired to the GED, we did not lower standards between grade levels. We guided students in mastery of sequential techniques and the importance of foundational skills that would insure easy access to the knowledge needed for GED.

Many students achieved the GED. All students were encouraged to become self-directed, but some surpassed all expectations in mastering materials.

I can't describe the educational stimulation and learning experience I had setting up the learning lab for adults, but I can reiterate some valuable lessons that I learned while helping adults whose experience in life had been varied and less than tranquil.

I learned that Adult Basic Education is one of the paradoxical problems of the twentieth century and that society will need to answer to this problem.

I believe that the single most effective teaching device available to a teacher and or a facilitator is his or her own educational preparation, behavior in the classroom, and attitude toward the students.

I am confident that all adult students want to feel accepted, respected, and supported when they are struggling with knowledge essential to their well being.

I observed that my students felt more "adult" in a friendly atmosphere that is trusting and free from "schoolish" rules and one in which I listened to what they had to say.

I learned that each student needs to have his or her future enhanced, ego nurtured, ability confirmed, and a clear understanding about how to proceed to achieve educational goals.

I recognized adult students as workers, spouses, parents, and citizens.

I am confident that we have the technology and the resources to meet the educational needs for the twenty-first century.

All of my adult students understood the logic behind the Adult Basic Education (ABE) learning lab type of teaching and learning if I analyzed thoroughly, explained fully, and led carefully.

My students were pleased when I secretively led them through the self-directed learning procedures where they, in fact, became responsible for their own learning with no restrictions or limitations.

I challenged all students to the next rung on the ladder. Many students achieved the Graduate Equivalency Diploma (GED) when they had very limited expectations of doing so when they enrolled. Being self-directed, many worked secretively for 85 percent mastery of materials.

I believed in a monitoring system that helped the staff and students to keep on "track" and that supports the students' efforts.

I considered it a privilege to create an educational program for adult students, some of whom failed in their earlier classroom experience or had to surrender to robots, while others were trying to keep pace with job entry level requirements and still others were returning to the halls of learning for self-enrichment.

I wanted to make sure that classroom management reflected students' needs—not the needs of the establishment. I no longer felt I needed to support the assembly line technology in teaching and learning. Moreover, I realized as never before the breadth and depth of my assignment. I could also reflect on my earlier training, feelings, and experience as a registered graduate nurse. Every decision that I made about a patient and every procedure that I carried out was for the good of the patient in treating a specific illness.

In 1972 the Adult Basic Education (ABE) program for Alcoa, Blount County, and Maryville Schools was evaluated by state of Tennessee Vocational Educational Evaluation Team's Coordinator, William Henry. Our program received commendations for the type of teaching, a highly motivated staff, the giving of free time when necessary, excellent newspaper coverage, increased enrollment, an efficient method of testing and evaluating of a student's performance, a monitoring system for each student, a totally individualized program of instruction provided to meet the needs of each adult student, and the continuing of my own education.

Student enrollment increased every year. Satellite programs were established in the county's schools, in housing units, and in the jail.

It was amazing to me how many drop-outs returned to the Adult Learning Center to get their GED. I was further pleased when adults with grown children who had been out of school for years came for help. Many parents came to get help with the most basic reading skill so they could help their children with school work.

The question has been asked, how can adults, without basic education skills, change their lives and be able to participate in the greatest document ever written? (the Declaration of Independence)? This is how one adult student solved her problem:

Betty was fifty-three years old and had worked for many years as a nurse's aide and home health aide. She had finished the eighth grade in 1943 and remembered that a high school education was not necessary for a good job at that time.

However a few years ago, Betty could not find employment as an aide because she did not have a high school diploma. She finally found employment in a local factory, but her position did not fulfill her personal needs. A major lay-off at the factory ultimately led to her discovery of Adult Basic Education.

"I knew I had to have a high school diploma to get a job I would enjoy. I saw the sign, 'Adult Basic Education—Learning Lab', on the fence at the Everett campus every day when I took my youngest son to school," she remembered.

One day she decided to give the ABE classroom a try. In Betty's own words, "Walking through the doors wasn't an easy thing to do. But when I walked in, I was greeted by one of the instructors and my fears disappeared. Every one was so helpful, I knew I was in the right place."

Betty remembered the day she took her GED at the University of Tennessee as another turning point in her life: "I remember sitting on the bench on Cumberland Avenue waiting for the three o'clock bus. I said to myself, 'I can do anything I want to do now that I have my diploma'. I decided that going back home could wait a few hours, and I walked through the buildings at the University dreaming of all the possibilities that were open to me."

Betty chose to follow an educational path that would lead to a career in nursing. Her next step was to enroll in a nursing assistant's class at Blount Occupational Educational Center (BOEC). The knowledge and experience she gained in this part-time educational program "improved on her dreams."

Betty credits her instructors in the GED and BOEC programs with encouraging her to apply for the Licensed Practical Nurse (LPN) class offered by BOEC on the Everett campus. Betty completed the LPN classes, took and passed the Tennessee State Board Licenser test, and is employed full-time at Blount Memorial Hospital.

Enthusiastically, she explained what the LPN program means to her: "The training I received opens a variety of career opportunities. Nursing is a profession where you can tell people you care about them, love them. This is important to me and gives me the satisfaction I want from a career."

Betty's family has been supportive of her efforts. Her husband and four sons, ages thirty-four, thirty-two, twenty-eight, and ten, are interested in her accomplishments and help her any way they can. "My family tells me to go study, and they ask about my grades. Our family life has changed—it is even better than before."

Betty sums up her experience with adult education: "A high school diploma opens so many doors; mine has brought me a great deal of happiness. The key to where I am today is the day I walked into the ABE classroom on the Everett campus in Maryville, Tennessee. I hope other adults are aware of the educational opportunities in Blount County."

This case study has been duplicated many times in the Adult Basic Education learning lab type of teaching/learning.

The joy of my Appalachian journey led me along a changing path in which I experienced both sides of the gold coin. I believe R. G. Des Dixon in *Future Schools* said it best.

> In an earlier era most people could parent successfully because society was simpler: children worked alongside parents or surrogates; job skills were learned by watching and helping; the family was a complete economic and social unit; literacy was unnecessary; change was almost non-existent; pace was slow; people lived entire lives in one place; support was all around in the extended family and stable village; parenting behavior was learned by osmosis, observation and imitation.
>
> Not any more. Society is now complex: parents and children are separated by work and interests; literacy is essential; jobs and job training are beyond family control; change is constant; the extended family is gone; people move often; neighbors are strangers; pace is frantic; there is no accessible model of parenting and no training. [4]

[4.] Dixon, R.G. Des *Future Schools*, ECW Press Toronto, Ontario: 1992 pp 313-314.

I have always been proud that Appalachia offers opportunities to people who want to persevere. Betty wanted to persevere, and today she is an indispensable member of the health care team at Blount Memorial Hospital.

This is a typical Adult Basic Education classroom at the Alcoa, Blount County, and Maryville School system.

Chapter Twelve

Retirement

Through necessity, people in Appalachia have changed their life styles, work ethic, and standard of living. Every age is an age of change, for the world never stands still. Likewise, change in the twentieth century has raced across time and left the world trembling. The past seems to be crumbling and the shape of the future has not yet become clear.

Retirement for Elgin and me was different than it was for our parents and grandparents. As a young adult, I remember that retirement was an extension of life's activities. When an elderly couple could no longer perform tasks essential for living, a meaningful life was over and they painfully waited until life for them would end.

By contrast, people today have a pre-arranged retirement plan with choices of early retirement or semi-retirement that allows income for retirement living.

This allows flexibility, freedom, choice, and time to do things of interest before old age "sneaks" in, that would otherwise never have gotten done.

In 1981, Elgin and I were still working, but we were dangerously close to retirement age. One of our concerns was our house—a three-floor house plan is not particularly designed for elderly. We had talked about remodeling, but it seemed that anything we would do would ruin the design and not accomplish our objective—a floor plan self-contained on one floor. If we decided to build, an interesting solar design weighed heavily on Elgin's mind.

On Saturdays after teaching and going to school all week, I would clean the three floors to a sparkling glitter. Every time I did this it seemed a little less necessary and a little more of an imposition. And the only time Elgin and I had to talk over our retirement needs was during the evening meal. We took turns bringing up the subject when one or both of us had had a busy day and longed for peace and quiet. The treatment was total silence or a negative comment. This went on for several months, and finally when Elgin again brought up the subject, I said, "It is time to stop talking about selling or building; we need to do something!"

The next day at the Kwanis Club, Elgin talked to Ken Millsaps, an architect, about his experience in building solar houses. That evening Elgin sketched a solar house plan and explained in detail the downstairs floor plan. I was shocked but pleased. Elgin said, "Building a house will take ten years out of my life, but we will build our retirement home."

Ken had a degree in architectural design and one in engineering. At that time, a solar house to me was a hole in the ground with a sod roof. Elgin, however, with his curiosity about solar energy and his scientific mind, equipped himself to work with Ken in the understanding of how to use the sun's rays to heat our house.

During the time of our indecisiveness, we decided to purchase a lot in the Turnberry subdivision—one that would lend itself to passive or active solar heat.

It was in the early fall when Elgin, Ken, and I had our first meeting to discuss the solar heating aspects versus conventional heating. With pride, Elgin faced Ken with his design and spelled out the self-contained features that we wanted on the first floor. Ken met with us many times and exposed us to many floor plans before we finally decided on the one we have lived in for fifteen years now.

When the blueprints were almost finished, we invited Ed Hummel, the contractor, to meet with us. The day came when Ed positioned the house on the lot and staked off the floor plan. The next step was the bulldozer scooping out a space for the clean, crushed rock for the active part of the solar system. It did seem unreal to me that we were going to sell our house that had served us so beautifully for thirty years and go through the agony of building a retirement home.

Incidentally, the children felt the same way, but more so. When we told them we were going to sell and build they were shocked and less than pleased. They were serious about not wanting us to sell "their" house. At that time they had their own houses. But they wanted the house they knew best to be there for them forever. Bit by bit they became reconciled, and as time passed curiosity got the best of them. We kept the phone busy and the trips home were more frequent.

Elgin brought the project into focus when he suggested using Indiana limestone for the exterior framing. We had talked about what to use and tentatively decided on brick. However, Elgin had a meeting in Indianapolis and on the way up he pointed out commercial buildings and dwellings made from Indiana limestone. It was a dark gloomy day and I wasn't all that impressed. However, Elgin ordered materials from several quarry establishments, and when I learned that one could choose from several random patterns I was more interested.

Terry Huffstetler was on the job as chief carpenter. He was busy reading blueprints and securing supplies at the lumber yard. Elgin and I had taken pictures of the furniture (antiques handed down through the families) that we wanted to keep. We would need some living room furniture and perhaps furniture for the master bedroom on the first floor. We had a meeting with Henry Law, an interior decorator, and he did a portfolio of needs. Periodically Elgin and I would go down and make choices of needed items, including carpeting and wallpaper.

Kenneth Cleveland custom built the cabinets for the bathroom, kitchen, and laundry room.

One beautiful October day, Elgin and I visited the Indiana limestone quarries. I was surprised and pleased at the showroom exhibits of size, width, and length and smooth-faced, etched, or scarred choices of stone to choose from. In addition, they had a mock-up outside of every conceivable design displaying glitter in the bright sunshine and autumn leaves. We chose the random patterns with a scarred face. I was humbled to think our retirement home would be made from the glittering limestone from Elgin's home state. Indiana is noted for limestone that has been shipped around the world.

Things got off to a slow start. I was reminded that this would be the case until the workmen got the house under roof, which might be sometime around Christmas.

Elgin and I would eat dinner and then rush over to see what the workers had accomplished during the day. Sometimes we could identify some progress, but for the most part it was the same as the day before. They did not work on rainy days.

The first load of stone came in March of 1982. I can't remember when the stone mason from Gatlinburg came to face the outside and fireplace wall inside. For Elgin and me, this was a "show and tell" situation. The mason brought his own help and it was fascinating to watch them chip a stone so it would be in harmony or contrast with the one beside it.

We didn't have to ask the question about when we would get in the house. It was self-evident that it would be fall of the year or later. We learned early on to be a little more patient and to keep up with our commitment to our respective laboratories, and time would take care of our eager expectations.

It was time for me to review my teaching schedule and see for sure when I wanted to give notice of my retirement. After school started, I wrote Mr. Charles Bean, Director of Vocational Education, and informed him of my plans to retire in the spring of 1983. This meant that I would work one year after moving into the house. Elgin was going to work until 1987.

When the children left the 1215 Oak Park home, they failed to take all their belongings with them. Each of the three bedrooms upstairs had attic storage under the rafters, and a long attic space the length of the hallway was filled with musical instruments, clothing, scout equipment, and memorabilia belonging to Beccie, Richard, Johanna, and Ella.

Elgin spent a full day cleaning out the storage bins and carrying plunder to the basement which eventually filled all four corners which had been labeled Beccie, Richard, Johanna, and Ella. We invited them for the weekend and asked them to bring the largest conveyance they had in which to put their belongings. They began to filter in about ten o'clock Friday night and it was well after midnight before the laughs, yells, and screams ended. They relived their past and had forgotten about how much stuff they had stored.

Richard, against all odds, had the most. He saved all his school work, charts, science projects, math papers, and themes. Scouting, hiking, boating, horse equipment, and scuba diving equipment filled the basement closets.

To make this occasion more memorable, we had a backyard barbecue Saturday afternoon. Between times they did some swapping and shopping and managed to get their conveyances loaded.

Long before the house was finished, Elgin and I separated furnishings that we could use in our retirement house and things that we could not use. Fortunately, Richard was furnishing his house and he could use furniture and appliances. Unfortunately there were other things, decorative and ornamental, that we couldn't use. It was necessary to have another weekend and conduct a silent auction. That was fun for the children, and a big relief for Elgin and me. Moreover, we had some items that went to the auction of the New Providence Church.

In spring of 1982, when the rains ceased and sun shone, the building crew worked every day on their own specialties, and we could see progress in the making. Elgin and I worked to keep ahead in choosing bathroom fixtures, appliances, locks and latches for doors and windows, drapes, bedspreads, carpet, wallpaper, and furniture.

On August 18, 1982 we moved into our new house. I shall never forget how considerate the movers were in getting everything placed correctly. They parked the moving van so they could use the sidewalk to the private entrance to the upstairs patio and to the upstairs bedrooms. All the furniture was massive antiques, and once placed it would be there for the duration. Henry Law supervised the downstairs and did a lot of the detailed work himself, upstairs and downstairs.

Within the month, we had a housewarming for all the people that had anything to do with the building of our retirement home. Between the chitchatting, eating, and sipping, the cameras were clicking, and we still have a group picture to tell the story.

We were listed in the fall Parade of Homes newsletter. Unfortunately, it was a rainy day, and we protected floors from muddy tracks as best we could but we were not fully successful.

When I retired in the spring of 1983, I was duly remembered with fun, food, and fellowship by the Blount County Adult Basic Education Department. Before we ate, a personal petition to the Creator that I might enjoy and be blessed in my retirement activities lifted my spirit. Tender thoughts were conveyed by an orchid. The engraved ABE gold pendant still brings back wonderful memories. The congratulatory letter from Lamar Alexander, then governor, was appreciated very much. Some of my students wrote letters to Dean Stone, the editor of the Maryville *Daily Times* in my behalf, and they appeared in section "Your Opinion." Dean Stone wrote an editorial in my behalf—"Adults can Appreciate Light of Knowledge"—under "Our Opinion." The kind remarks will never be forgotten.

Elgin and I had our respective hobbies during our lifetimes. I made the children's clothes and I made my own. I read a lot, especially when I was in school and teaching. It came as a surprise to me that my job called for a lot of writing. Reports, records, and the Tennessee State Department asked each section of the state to get out a quarterly newspaper about what we were doing and interesting things about the learning lab type of teaching, which was called *East Tennessee Adult Educator*. This was very beneficial in that we could find out about teaching techniques used by other school systems if they had an Adult Basic Educational department, and most did. The other bulletin, *The Educator*, was a publication known as the Tennessee Alliance for Continuing Higher Education (TACHE). They solicited news items and professional articles from staff members working in ABE departments. I was a charter member of this organization, and I enjoyed writing articles for *The Educator*.

I had a problem with the material that I saved during my twelve years of teaching and the information from three leading magazines to which I subscribed: *Educational Leadership, Phi Delta Kappan,* and *Harvard Review.* When I got all my material sorted out and placed in a file cabinet under headings and an index, I thought that would be the end of what I needed to do. In all honesty, I felt that I had some material that would be especially applicable to teachers, parents, school administrators, and for in-service training where programs need to be individualized for special needs. I just had to write a book titled Education: *The Plight of the Illiterate Adult.*

To keep up in the filed and to satisfy my own curiosity, I was a regular contributor from 1990 to 1994 to Educational Leadership: *For Supervision and Curriculum Development.*

Elgin, in addition to being a pathologist and director of the laboratory at Blount Memorial Hospital, is a serious genealogist and historian. During the years he did research on ancestral lines in the family. After retirement he converted his data and information into book form in an Ancestral Genealogy and Tour Guide: *of the Kintner Family.* Also, Elgin and Lorene

Smith authored *Blount County Remembered.* It depicted the 1890s photography of W.O. Garner who lived in Blount County at turn of the century. Proceeds from the sale were turned over to Blount county Library for the benefit of its genealogical collection. Elgin has written scientific articles for publication all during his professional life. In April 1971, the Association of Clinical Scientists presented Elgin with the Billings Medal. Elgin exhibited "A Simplified Approach to Acid/Base Balance" in the human body. His explanation was printed in scientific journals and as a chapter in medical textbooks to be used by medical students and pathologists in medical laboratories.

Our retirement years have been years of sheer enjoyment. We have been pleased with the solar feature that floods sunlight in the great room and the three upstairs bedrooms during the winter months. We have a gas furnace for back up heat when the stored heat is depleted. We have so much sunshine in the winter time that the system is financially desirable, not to speak of the unusually satisfying warm feeling for those whose lives are marching on.

Our house surpassed our lofty expectations in convenience, space, and comfortable living. The house is easy to maintain, and so far there have been no big repair jobs or remodeling.

Retirement has allowed us to do sightseeing trips, long weekends, and entertain company from far and near. It was especially nice for us and convenient for our friends from Indiana and Virginia to stop for a visit on route to Florida for the winter.

In May of 1995, Elgin and I went on the Pennsylvania German Heritage Tour with Dr. Don Yoder, a professor of religious studies in the department of folklore and folklife at the University of Chicago. He also offers courses in American Civilization.

We spent weeks preparing ourselves for this trip. Elgin's interest in genealogy and my interest in Christendom, particularly the early settlers in Pennsylvania and the western movement, called for reading, researching, and familiarizing myself with the thirteen-day trip circling the Rhineland and the Swiss Alps.

When we got home, we each did a journal of the Pennsylvania German Heritage Tour which was comprised of thirty-two people, including group pictures taken at Heidelberg Castle. We have many other pictures that illustrated where we had been and what we saw. The pictures make the script in our memory log come alive.

I might add that our daughter Beccie and son-in-law Rufus King met us at Belfast, Ireland, to visit some mutual friends and take a picture of Elgin's great-grandmother's stone house.

Elgin and I are continuing to keep the text writers busy. We are converting memorabilia into human interest stories. This being Tennessee's two-hundredth year of statehood, we have pictures and articles of the Kintner family and the Pritchett family in *The History of Blount County, Tennessee, and Its People, 1795-1995* and in *Jefferson County, Tennessee Families and History, 1792-1996.*

As part of Tennessee's statehood celebration, I was listed among the First Families of Tennessee through the Pritchett/Bowman relationship. I consider this important information for my children and grandchildren. They all have a copy. They can pass the torch to my great-grandchildren.

Living in the heart of Appalachia, Elgin and I have had a wonderful time raising our children: Beccie King, Richard Kintner, Johanna Bryant, and Ella Brown. The recreational opportunities in the Great Smoky Mountains national Park, the network of lakes created by the Tennessee Valley Authority, Oak Ridge with the research/science laboratory, and the Museum of Appalachia offer cultural and educational opportunities unequaled. The attractions of Gatlinburg are exciting and adventurous.

Each girl's wedding with each new in-law was a cherished addition to the Kintner family. Each grandson was special and added fun and enjoyment untold. Beccie and Rufus gave us Kevin and Brad King. Of course Grandma and Grandpa Kintner have been in ecstasy ever since. A few years later Ella and Tom gave us Micah and Caleb Brown, which added rapture to our state of ecstasy.

Elgin and I enjoyed Kevin's and Brad's weddings to the point where we felt blessed indeed. They both have beautiful, loving wives, and good jobs, and we couldn't ask for anything more. However, some day, I want to be a great-great grandma. Micah and Caleb are moving along, and my greatest hope is to see them through school, married, and with a home of their own like Kevin and Brad. Boys, somewhere along the way somebody must have some granddaughters!

My Appalachian journey was a venture into the unknown. I have lived, loved, and learned with every step along the way. My pilgrimage has been marked with the characteristic of trying to understand the sophistication of our culture, no matter where on the "space ship Earth" one lives.

I have felt the pain of those that experience poverty, hunger, and hopelessness.

I am especially grateful for my parents' guidance and the passing on of their spiritual heritage. I am grateful for an extended loving family and especially Elgin, my husband, who cleared many a roadblock for me along the way.

My life has been filled with an avalanche of change, but by the grace of God I have been strengthened through ordinary people, the insignificant, and the imperfect.

Our solar retirement home.

Family picture. Front row, left to right: Elgin Kintner, Tom Brown, Johanna Bryant holding Caleb Brown, me, Beccie King and Micah Brown. Back row: Brad King, Larry Bryant, Richard Kintner, Ella Brown, Kevin King, and Rufus King.